Conversations with the Spirit World

souls who have ended their lives
speak from above

Lysa Moskowitz-Mateu

Channeling Spirits Books

Los Angeles

Channeling Spirits Books

ISBN# 0-9707468-6-5

Library of Congress Card Number# 2001086377

Channeling Spirits World Wide Website Address is
www.channelingspirits.com

Telephone: 310-820-0711 or 310-650-SOUL
E-Mail: channelingspirits@hotmail.com

This Book

is Dedicated

to the Freedom

of your Spirit

and the Fulfillment

of your Soul

Thank You....

As I sit here thinking of which combination of words will best express the love and gratitude I feel for the people in my life, I am reminded that it is not words which will convey the depth of my emotion, it is the actions I take in allowing those whom I love to know, feel, and experience my love for them. And yet, since this is a book, I think a few words will do....

Thank you to my parents, Lenny & Linda, for being what every child hopes and prays their parents will be. You are that, and so much more. Thank you for loving and supporting me during every second of my life. It is a privilege to call you my parents.

Thanks Mom for not freaking out when your friend told you your house was filled with spirits as I was writing this book.

Thank you to my brother, David, for being open to everything I bring forth and for supporting me and being proud of who I am, regardless of how many times I stormed in your room as a kid.

Thank you Siobhan, my golden retriever, for snoring faithfully beneath my desk as I typed these words, and for reminding me that although work is important, so is play.

Thank you: Simon Dabkowsi and Robin Gailes, for your expertise and talent in assisting me with the cover. Martin Mercer and Michael Ames, for your energy and support. Anita Stuppler, Anette Craig, and Johnny Gillespie, for your inspired actions and belief in the importance of getting this book out to the world.

And most of all, I thank with every ounce of my soul, my husband Satori Mateu, for igniting the passion of my spirit and for loving me each day as if it were the first. I love you from my smallest pinky toe to above my head into the cosmos. It is a privilege and a gift to share life with you.

Thank you Charley. You know why....

Also available in 2001 by Lysa Moskowitz-Mateu

BOOKS

Opening the Door to the Other Side
(pre-order your copy now of Lysa's autobiography)

Conversations with my Dog

**Someday My Prince Will Come
and Other Fairy Tales**

You Are a Gift to the World

Diary of a Bulimic

Now You're Cookin'
(Recipes for success)

AUDIO TAPES

Conversations with the Spirit World
(complete book on tape – Available Now!)

Building a Bridge to the Other Side
(Mediumship Development Series. Available Now!)

Psychic Development – levels 1,2,3

Advanced Mediumship Development

Psychic Self- Defense

Lessons in Psychometry

Meeting & Working with your Spirit Guides

FEATURE FILM

Journey From Within

*To order books, tapes, seminars, and channeling sessions
with Lysa, log onto www.channelingspirits.com
Or call 310-820-0711*

You Have a Voice That is Meant to be Heard

THE BEGINNING

Saturday, November 6, 1999.

I sit at my computer.

Place my fingers on the keyboard.

And the words, "*What were you thinking right before you killed yourself?*" come across the screen.

What follows is 11 days of typing 135 words a minute, whereupon I ask questions and receive answers from 17 souls who have committed suicide.

Everything that is written was written in a stream of higher consciousness or whatever the particular term best describes the awesome events that colored my life since I first began writing about the subject of suicide and sanity in the fall of 1998.

First let me backtrack to where this all began....

At the beginning.

March 15, 1995

I am standing at the intersection of Montana Avenue and San Vicente Boulevard in Brentwood, California. I am trying to decide whether to study my French literature in translation at The Coffee Bean or Starbucks.

I choose Coffee Bean.

The reason is immediately apparent.

Soft brown eyes, plump juicy lips, a face like an Adonis. I am in love. In a few moments, I will come to know him as Charley.

Right now, he is God.

"Would you like some Pepto-Bismol?" the Adonis asks as he peers at the book I am reading -- *Nausea* by Jean Paul Sartre. He slides past me and disappears into the men's room.

A man much too old to be working as a coffee clerk leans over to my table and whispers, "He likes you. I watched his face as he spoke to you. It was red with passion. You and him will be together."

"That's impossible," I reply. "I'm married."

"My grandfather was a Shaman," he continues. "He passed along his psychic abilities to me. You and Charley will be together. I'm telling you this because I

2

want you to know that there are no accidents. Everything that is meant to happen - does. You two will be together."

Charley comes out of the men's room and stares at me... through me.

I am going to throw up.

We are so connected. It is strong. Intense.

You will be together... My grandfather was a shaman... There are no accidents.

Later that evening, I telephone the Coffee Bean and ask Charley for a date.

"Tonight," he says. "Let's go out tonight."

How can I go out tonight? What will I tell my husband David? I can't do this! I cannot risk ruining my marriage over a John Stamos look-a-like.

"Okay, " I blurt out. "What time?"

7:00 p.m.
Charley enters my car.
I want to kick him out.
He smells too good.
He looks too good.
He's acting much too happy to see me.
He's dangerous.
I have more to lose than he does.

"This looks like a good movie," he says pointing to the newspaper. "Hideaway," it's called.

How Perfect.

The next day, Charley and I are sitting outside Starbucks on 3rd Street Promenade in Santa Monica and we see the Shaman guy. I run over to him, thinking he'll be excited that his prophecy came true. But he just looks at me, with glazed over eyes and a crooked smile. Later I find out he got fired from Coffee Bean. No one knows where he went, where he came from, or even… if he exists.

So Charley and I spend the next six months sharing our dreams, revealing our souls, watching the moonlight from his balcony and pondering the meaning of life and death. I file for divorce.

Charley takes me away to Santa Barbara on a romantic getaway. To lighten up my mood he covers his head with a white sheet and informs tourists that he is a very rich oil sheik and owns the beach on which they walk.

At night, he plays piano for me at the hotel bar then serenades me to sleep playing his Gordalin.

As my eyes close, he whispers I love you and in that moment, I am transported to another realm of existence; one in which I had never visited before.

I will not go into the details of why I finally broke up with Charley. I will just say that he did not take it lightly.

You see, Charley was a tortured soul. Self-tortured. He was brilliant, relentless, passionate, introspective, and mad. One night, he left the number of a funeral home on my pager. I guess it was his twisted way of telling me he needed help.

Charley lived by his impulses.

I lived by my heart.

He wanted to run from his feelings.

I wanted to understand mine.

So we parted ways and my life went on.

I met and married my current husband, Satori, and my life became about integrity and honesty, inspiration and dedication. It became about reaching, arriving, celebrating, wondering, asking, searching, and understanding that ultimately, we don't know.

Ultimately, we must trust.

Why am I here? What is it I was born to do?

To be? To contribute? To learn?

The answers came in the quiet moments between the dawn of a new day and the darkening of the sky. The moments when I stopped and noticed what was going on around me, inside me, inside of someone else.

My relationship with Charley took me to places I had not visited for a long time. It took me to gut-wrenching pain and indescribable ecstasy, infectious laughter, goofiness, energy, exhilaration, introspection, self-destruction, and love... so much love, and pain... so much pain… and happiness. The kind of happiness that lifted me out of bed in the morning with only a few hours sleep and gave me the motivation and desire to go beyond where I'd ever gone before; to live at a level of intensity most would find uncomfortable.

September 1998

I am walking along Montana Avenue in Santa Monica and a familiar voice shouts out my name. I see Jonathan, Charley's father, sitting at a café. He asks me to join him.

"I only have a moment," I tell him.

He looks uncomfortable in my presence.

I ask him how things are going.

He says they're going well.

"I drove by your apartment two months ago. Charley was sitting outside smoking a cigarette. I was going to stop by and say hello, but I knew Satori, my husband, would not have liked it.

You know how Charley is. He's not one to keep his hands off a married woman," I laugh.

"You couldn't have seen Charley two months ago," Jonathan says.

"Well, maybe it was three. But I saw him, sitting on that chaise lounge outside the house."

"No," he continues, his face turning white. "CHARLEY'S DEAD."

"Excuse me?" I ask, understanding precisely what he said.

"He committed suicide a year ago."

I am speechless.

There is a split second where the lines between what you now know and what you're about to learn, exist. Once you cross that line, your life is never the same again. You forever refer to it in terms of, "before you found out" and "after you found out."

I was about to cross that line.

"How did he die?"

"He jumped off the Lincoln Boulevard overpass onto the Santa Monica freeway. He landed onto a Vintage Porsche. Just like Charley, to choose the most expensive car," he jokes, trying to fend off the pain.

We laugh. A moment of remembrance in Charley's honor allowed us the freedom to laugh.

And then, we cry.

7

"I tried to get a hold of you when Charley died, but you weren't listed."

"When did it happen?" I ask.

"On November 1, 1996. All Soul's Day.

His memorial service was November 10th."

"My birthday," I reply.

I could not comprehend that Charley was gone. Later that day I return home to find an envelope on my desk. "I received these photos in the mail today. I don't know who they're of, but he sure is good-looking," says a note from my mom.

I open the envelope and gasp when I see the face — it is Charley.

Two years prior, I had taken a roll of film that contained photos of Charley to the drug store to be developed. For some reason, I never picked them up.

My mother knew Charley. My mother had spent time with Charley during the six months we were virtually inseparable. Yet in these photos, she did not recognize his face. They were modeling photos and he looked quite different.

I felt spooked and curious about what this meant. Photos arrive the same day I find out Charley is dead. "What do you want me to know?" I ask the photos.

A few days later...

…The answer came.

"Write," a voice tells me.

"Write what?" I ask.

"Just write."

So for the next eight months, for 10-12 hours a day, I wrote, cried, laughed and explored untapped dimensions of my soul, pockets of who I was… pieces of who I was going to be. It was an incredible, exhilarating, enlightening, painful, and challenging experience, the result of which became my film, Journey From Within.

During the writing of this film, I had many "mystical" experiences. One night, a transparent image wearing something blue, ran across my mirror. I felt a spirit beside me. I called my dog over, but she wouldn't come. Her hair stood up straight and she growled fiercely.

The next moment, the lights went out. I got them back on and they went out again.

The next evening, I was feeling the presence of Charley and asked him to send me a sign. I asked aloud so my husband could bare witness to anything that occurred. At the time I was reading a book I had never read before and when I turned the page, the first word on top was — Charlie.

Then, on Saturday, November 6, 1999, the words "*What were you thinking right before you killed yourself,*" spread across the screen.

This is the story of 17 souls who have something to say.

I am just the vehicle through which they chose to speak.

In reading this, you are listening...

and allowing them to finally be heard.

Lysa Moskowitz-Mateu
December 1, 1999
5:08 p.m. Santa Monica, CA
With my dog Siobhan snoring loudly on the floor.

10

WHO THEY ARE

Except for Charley, I had no prior knowledge of any of the people who spoke through me. Full names, dates, causes of death were verified through researching the information received in the writing. I have left out the last names to protect the privacy of the families. Some simply revealed themselves to me, but did not offer any words in the text.

1. CHARLEY: 1/15/73—11/1/96—jumped off Lincoln
Boulevard/Santa Monica Freeway Overpass. **Age:** 22

2. ANGELA: died November 11   **Age:** 16

3. ALEXY: 11/7/75   6/24/96— hung himself. **Age:** 20

4. JOSEPH: died 11/20/97—shot himself. **Age:** 35

5. JOHN: 11/14/62—9/28/98. **Age:** 35

6. BEAU: died in 1998 - Shot himself. **Age:** 12

7. NANCY: died in 1999-Shot herself. **Age:** 35

8. SEAN: died 1996—Shot himself. **Age:** 29

9. JAY: 11/14/64-died in 1999—Hung himself. **Age:** 35

10. BRETT: Died in 1984. **Age:** 15

11. JOSHUA: Carbon monoxide poisoning. **Age:** 15

12. MICHAEL: Shot himself. **Age:** 35

13. GARY: **Age:** 27

14. ARTHUR: No information

15. JESS: 11/27/69—6/13/97. Drove off freeway. **Age:** 27

16. KIMBERLY: 11/5/74—12/31/95. Overdosed. **Age:** 20

17. JEFFREY: died in 1992. Overdosed. **Age:** 51

THE CONVERSATION

What were you thinking right before you killed yourself?

KIMBERLY (age 20): I was feeling despondent and afraid. Actually, it took a long time to muster up the courage to go ahead with my plan. I was looking for someone to talk me out of it. I was begging someone to see the pain I was in. I cannot blame them, but I do think the signs were there; signs that most people aren't attuned to looking for.

What would have made a difference for you?

If someone had spoken to me, really took the time and spoke to me, not like a victim or a defective piece of machinery, but as a person going through pain. I think then I would have chosen to live.

When did you first feel life wasn't worth living?

When I was five.

I used to play with my sister and her friends. They teased me. The girls were really mean. They pulled my hair and called me names. I came home crying, bawling actually. My mother did nothing. She looked at me with a sympathetic 'poor dear' attitude and just turned away. I remember feeling my life had no point; that I was insignificant and people were mean just to be mean and adults, the ones who were supposed to know it all, really didn't know anything at all. Yeah, they knew information and stuff, but they didn't really <u>know</u>. You know what I mean?

They really didn't know me... who I was, how much I loved people and animals, especially my cats. They didn't know how much I cared and they didn't care to ask. My mother refused to acknowledge the signs, the ones that yelled to her late at night or cried like a newborn baby under the covers in my bed. I was in so much pain, but what I didn't know then, that I do know now, was that I, and only I, was the creator of all that pain.

What do you mean by that?

I did it to myself.

Sure, other people did things to me, but I was responsible for how I interpreted and held onto their actions. I was responsible for the things I told myself after they and their actions were long gone.

What did dying teach you?

JESS (age 27):

Dying taught me that there is no death.

Yeah, my body is gone.

But I feel more connected to the earth plane now than I ever have.

I still walk with souls who live in a body.

I still connect with the people whom I connected with before. The only difference is -- they cannot see me, and well, according to them, this makes all the difference in the world. The pain I feel at not being able to let them know I am there—or rather, not being able to break through their veil of certainty which says I cannot be there because I am dead, torments my soul even more now than when I was alive.

When I was alive, I wanted to be invisible.

Now that I am dead, I feel more visible than ever and just when I want people to see me

    -- They cannot.

What would have saved your life?

BEAU (age 12): Being listened to, or rather, listening to myself and others—listening to what they were doing to help me instead of what I thought they were doing to hurt me.

I was so critical when I was alive; critical of myself and my parents and everyone who dared to walk in my path.

I pushed so many people away when I was alive. I hate saying that word alive because I feel more alive now than I felt before I died. *This is not because I died.* It is because I learned how I should have lived when I was alive, when I had the chance to really make a difference.

Oh how I would do anything to be given another chance at life.

You see, from where I am, I cannot affect people or impact them in the same way I could have done when I lived inside a body.

I am forced to restrain myself as a spirit because beings in bodies do not delight in seeing spirits walk in the night.

What is your advice for those in pain?

CHARLEY (age 22): Snap out of it!

Just kidding, but not really. What I learned the moment my body was transported off the highway and into the morgue was –

I am not my body.

Now most of you are probably thinking I am quite slow to have just discovered this so late in the game, but really, I thought I *was* my body.

Whilst on earth I spent a hell of a lot of time adorning it, buying it things. Oh how so very important things were to my life. I lived for things— the buying of things, the giving of them, yet you know what's so funny?

I looked forward to dying so I could give up my things. They became the burden of my life instead of the pleasure. I felt burdened by having to play along with believing that things were the answer. I don't know how else to explain it except that I truly thought that things were going to make me happy.

It's true that anything can seemingly fill you up for a short time. But in the long run, what you don't take with you to heaven, you don't need to spend all of your time focusing on down there.

The same things you need on earth are the same things you need in heaven — love, connection, compassion, passion, you know, whatever.

That word whatever is looked upon so distastefully up here. The higher spirits actually detest it, so of course I started saying 'whatever' a lot. You say 'whatever' when you don't really want to say what's going on. Whatever is an excuse for not fully expressing whatever is behind whatever. Whatever is meant to mean "I DON'T CARE," but that's the big joke because we always care.

Always.

And the more we attempt to make it like we don't, the more we do. It's the big game of pretend that's going on right now in your world. It's cool to act like nothing matters when in reality -- it does.

I still like to relate to myself as being part of the human race. I forget, or choose to give up remembering, that I gave up that right a long time ago. I gave up the privilege to call myself a human being long before I died.

I actually died long before I died, if you know what I mean. I gave up living fully when all of those doctors told me that I was a sick human being in need of constant medication and help.

I gave up being who I am and became someone I am not. I became someone who did not resemble ME. I became everything they told me to be. I was smart when they said to be smart and funny when they demanded I be funny. Sometimes, just to piss them off, I would be funny when they demanded smart and smart when they demanded funny or I would be none of the above and just sit like a vegetable.

I would just sit and watch them scurry about looking for ways to make me talk, searching for the remedy that would bring me back to my senses.

What they didn't know was that I was at my senses the entire time. I knew exactly how to get myself into different states, yet I didn't let them know that I knew how to do this.

Why not?

Then they would win and take the credit for my spontaneous recovery. They would give credit to the pill they prescribed or their therapeutic techniques.

They would take all the credit away from me. Fuck that! I deserve some credit for all the shit I have put myself through during my lifetime. I take credit for the shit. I deserve credit for the good times as well. But nooo, doctors love to take the credit when you do something that has nothing to do with what they did.

I'm sorry. I apologize. I was just informed by my higher spirit that I am rambling on like an asshole. He, my higher spirit, didn't say the word asshole. He said, muttering idiot or babbling idiot, something like that. I put in the word asshole. I think it rather describes my behavior much better.

I am questioning whether I am writing this or you are writing it through me. How will I know for sure?

Are your hands sweaty?

Yes

Are they cold and clammy?

Yes.

Are you feeling like the words can't come out fast enough, like your fingers long to hit the typewriter keys at an ever faster pace and if you timed yourself, you would surely be hitting the keys at over 100 words per minute?

Yes.

Case closed.

SEAN (age 29):   Lysa, hello my name is Sean. I am here because you invited me here. I know you want to help all the kids who are in pain. I commend you for your efforts.

Thank you....

CHARLEY: You know, one thing I don't miss about the human world is the big dilemmas. Up here, we don't have them. The higher spirits teach us to call everything an opportunity.

SEAN: There's a woman pressing through right now. She wants to speak.

ANGELA (age 16):   Hello Lysa, I'm Angela. Angie in Heaven.

Not Angie on earth?

ANGIE: Never! My mother especially hated me being called Angie. She said it made me sound like a slut.

Lysa, I want you to know that I love you for what you are doing, for your commitment to helping others see the light. It is so dark on earth right now, so cold and dark. I feel afraid for you earthlings, even though the higher spirits tell me I should not feel afraid, yet I see what goes on and I feel afraid for the love you have lost.

It takes so much for you to love, just love another human being, not for what they do, not even for who they are to you, but just because to love is the right thing to do.

This is the love I speak of so often in heaven. This is the love I looked to others to give me. My mistake was in thinking I could get from the outside, that which was already inside of me.

I am afraid for the souls who seem so certain about what they know. They know what they know is right and leave no room for learning or discovery. It is good to have certainty, but too much certainty leaves you with a closed door. And who can walk through a closed door? Well whom, besides me?

I feel you and Satori have so much to give, so much goodness in your heart. Just as Martin Luther King, Jr., Gandhi, JFK, and others who have walked the path of enlightened living, you are burdened with the thought that you have to do something, go somewhere or change your environment or your surroundings in an attempt to find what you think you lack inside. But you don't.

All you need is right there inside of you. Don't you see it? God how I wish I could have seen it when I was alive. Maybe next time around, huh?

Yes. Next time around for sure.

November 6, 1999

Tonight as Satori and I were coming out from seeing the film, The Bone Collector, a blonde woman with a belly button ring, a long black skirt, and flowing blonde hair, asked me what movie I was coming from. I told her which one and she replied, "I am totally freaked out," and walked away.

I told Satori what the woman had said and he asked, "Are you going to just stand there or are you going to say something to her."

I felt the wave of apprehension shoot through my veins as I descended on the escalator. This was one of those moments. My word is to help those in pain. This woman told me she was freaked out. She was obviously in pain. What if I found out the next day that she had committed suicide, how would I feel then?

I went into the bathroom and found her there. I asked if she was okay. "Five years ago I was held captive by a crazed man. The movie brought back horrid memories. I couldn't see it."

I told her she didn't have to sit through a film she did not desire to see. "The guy who held me captive, he went to jail. I feel good about that because he was a serial killer. But now I'm going to have nightmares for days after seeing this film." I told her how to do a technique I use with my clients to change how they picture negative memories. I told her that I came in here specifically looking for her. Her face lit up with awe and appreciation. She told me she was so grateful I had done that.

November 7, 1999

NANCY (age 35): My name is Nancy. I was born in Massapequa, New York, which some people think is upstate, but it's not.

I have two sisters and one brother. And all of us are nuts. But I was the nuttiest nut of all. For fun, I would climb on my rooftop at night and shout to the neighbors, naked mind you, "I am Queen of all Massapequa! I have come to save your soul!"

Most people would laugh when they saw me, others would bow their heads low and pretend not to stare. The boys stared. Martin Pernicle stared. He thought seeing me naked on the rooftop was a ticket to see me naked in his bed, without my permission.

Rape, you call it down there. I used to call it rape when I was alive. Up here, there is no rape.

There is what there is. There is the fact that this boy touched my breasts and fondled my nipples and put his penis into me.

There is the fact I said no. The fact he said yes. The fact I cried all night from the ache in my groin. There is the fact I was no longer a virgin. The fact my mom told me to swear not to tell anyone. The fact I obeyed her command. But rape, no, that didn't happen, although at the time it was an adequate label to describe the things that had occurred.

When did you kill yourself?

24

I didn't. That's the big disappointment, the biggest joke of all.

I'm not dead.

CHARLEY: Denial. She's in denial.

NANCY: Am not.

BEAU: She's new here.

NANCY: Shut up. Why won't men ever shut up? On earth, they were silent. Here - they suddenly have so much to say.

CHARLEY: She's in the LA-LA Land of Limbo. She's not quite grasped the idea that her life is
                    but
              a
         dream.

CHARLEY: It happened to me.
        When I first died, I felt I wasn't dead. No way I could be dead with all the vivid images and pictures of those I loved racing before me in a sudden burst of memory. I saw everyone... everything... Every feeling, thought, and experience I had ever felt in my entire life,

I saw in one fell swoop... a flash of light before my eyes. It was an awesome display of the love I had shared and the people I had touched... and the pain I had caused.

I was standing right next to my father when he heard of my death.

I saw his face crinkle with despair.

I saw his upper lip quiver slightly.

He called my mom and hastily left word of my death on her answering machine. "You do not leave a message that your son is dead on an answering machine. It is the surest way to serve the person who hears the message with a heart attack." I tried to get him to slam down the phone. I literally yelled in his ear "SLAM DOWN THE PHONE!"

Did he listen to me? Of course not.

Has he ever listened to me? No.

I was determined to get through to this guy, this man who had raised me, this man who had done everything he could to support me through thick and thin, and I'll admit most of it was thick.

I screamed, shouted, yelled, "I'm right here dad!! Look at me!! I'm right here!!"

His eyes darted - left, right. He looked up, then down, behind me, in front.

Then, he looked directly at me and cried.

His body racked with pain. His hands shook wildly, out of control. Years of pent up emotion came flowing in huge buckets from his eyes.

"Oh my God," I thought to myself.

"What have I done?"

The unthinkable.

I had taken away a life from my father.

I had taken away his son.

I sat beside him and bawled louder than he. I struck myself in the face several times, attempting to get out the pain I had caused this gentle man who had done nothing but love me from the time I was born.

I didn't see what happened next. My actions were so automatic, so blatantly carved from the pain of my soul that my energy caused a wooden dragon statue to come crashing to the floor. It tumbled on its side and its neck broke off. In that moment, I was transported upward, in a spiraling, spinning motion, to the world in which I now live.

I wanted to go back to the life I had chosen to leave.

But I could not.

I was stuck with my decision.

I had thought that life on the other side would be free from life as it were on earth. I now know that life is life, no matter where it occurs. And what better place to play it out than on earth, where I could have materialized the visions I had in my mind and impacted the world in a way that now, I cannot.

Lysa, when I was alive, I was not brave with you. I covered up that which was foremost on my mind and in my soul because I was too afraid to allow my feelings to get out of hand. I loved you more than I had ever loved before. I loved you so much that expressing my love for you felt incomprehensible and dangerous to the preservation of my soul.

Love is dangerous; this is what we are taught.

Love hurts. Love is not safe. This is the stupidest bit of advice I received whilst on earth.

Let me revise it for you...

Love is all there is.

What I learned the moment I died was this:

All of the love I had been storing up in my emotional piggy bank, saving up for the day when some woman would crack me open and get drenched with all my love, was the biggest mistake I made. I was a selfish, stupid, petty person on earth. I say this as no insult to myself. I say this with honor and dignity and grace, none of which I practiced enough on earth.

What I failed to recognize is that death is not what I thought it was. Here I was thinking I could out smart God or the Gods (there are many as I now have the privilege of knowing firsthand, not like those

mortals on earth who claim, with utter defying
certainty, that what they know is the truth. God is
Jesus. God is Buddha. You go to hell for your sins.
What I say to them ever so politely is, "Please shut the
fuck up until you get your ass up here and see for
yourself firsthand, what is really going on!")

What I learned, that Nancy would soon learn,
is that love never dies.

People never die.

Their bodies die.

But they... do not.

People do not realize the level of relationship
they can continue to have with the 'dead.' 'It ain't over
till it's over,' as Babe Ruth said.

'And it ain't never over,' as I now say.

The entire human race is playing a huge game
of telephone. You say something, someone interprets it
according to their frame of reference and belief system
and repeats it differently to someone else, who further
interprets it in their own way and so on.

Human communication is twisted and insane.
Even the best of us who study literature, linguistics,
languages of all sorts, fail to communicate the most
essential communication of all— that of our Soul.

Our soul longs to speak -- yet who cares to
listen? Not listen as in I'm hearing you, I hear what

you're saying, but listen in a way so that what you say is felt in the deepest recess of my being. This is not hokey-pokey, foo-foo talk.

I mean if we could just for an instant feel on earth, the love felt in heaven, the entire universe would be transformed. This is what I meant when I said Nancy does not accept that she's dead because to accept that fact would mean to accept what a mistake she made in thinking that death over life was a choice to be made by her.

What is the purpose of a body, if being in heaven feels so good; if the love you feel now transcends the love you felt while on earth?

JOSEPH (age 35): Well, hello there, Lysa. My name is Joey. Joseph. J.M. III. And what I say to you is this:

There is no power in death.

We, the dearly departed, cannot affect the world in the same way you can. You have this body, this encasing that carries you from place to place. From home, to work or school, to the gym or to the playground or the library, back home to your living room or to the bedroom or the mall, etc.

What you don't realize, or have not yet realized, is what an awesome thing it is to be in a body -- your

30

body. You can forever play dress-up, like Barbie or Ken, and make yourself to be however and whatever you choose to be.

You have this fallacy that happiness is a permanent state, like Florida or California. That once you get there, you can move in, settle down, and that's that, happiness is your newfound home. This, my dear sweet friends, is a crock of shit...

NANCY: That is not true! I have felt happiness for long periods of time in my life. There were times when I felt nothing else.

BEAU: Untrue.

JOSEPH: Beau is right. You felt happiness because you focused on things that made you feel happy, like a new boyfriend, am I right?

NANCY: Yes.

JOSEPH: There is no such thing as feeling one thing all of the time, that is my point. The only reason Nancy thought she felt happiness and only happiness for an extended period of time is because happiness is what she focused on.

I'm sure things went sour once and awhile, but she probably didn't focus on sourness for very long. Her mind became trained to look, to stay with and focus on what was working in her life rather than what was not. So now when she looks back on her life or that particular period of her life, all she sees is happiness. Nancy had lots of reasons NOT to be happy during that period, yet she chose to be.

NANCY: Yeah, until I stopped choosing to be.

JOSEPH: What people down there do not realize is that death is not death, the way they think it is, like taking an aspirin which will relieve your pain. The pain of taking your life far outweighs the pain of living your life. So what I want to say…

CHARLEY: Am saying…

JOSEPH: Am saying….

CHARLEY: Want is in the future.

JOSEPH: Thank you Charley. The world could have really used you. He keeps all of us on track with our language and speaking of what we perceive to be our truth. He is a master of sorts. You guys sure lost out on this gem of a man.

CHARLEY: I'm teary. My eyes are actually watering from your words Joseph. I am deeply touched. Will you marry me?

ANGIE: I feel like we're rambling on, going from one subject to the next, fragmenting our words, our stories, what we desire to say, in the hopes that Lysa..

JOSEPH: We are fragmented because Lysa is the first person to ever ask us why we ended our lives and what we needed in order not to do so. And we owe it all to Charley.
   Thank you Charley for contacting Lysa, for showing her the way and for leading us to her. For your efforts, we are and will eternally be, grateful.

ALL: Here, here!

CHARLEY: It's unanimous then…
                I am God.

JOSEPH: I'm clear about one thing for you Nancy.

NANCY: What is that?

JOSEPH: Your kids miss their mom.

NANCY: I'm awful. I'm awful. I'm awful. I'm awful.

JOSEPH: If you say so.

NANCY: Don't be a smart ass.

JOSEPH: How come? Because I am right and in being right it means…

NANCY: I am wrong.

JOSEPH: That's the biggest crock of bullshit I have ever heard. If I am right, I am right. Period. It doesn't mean anything about who or how you are. All it means is that I am right.

You don't need to find the personal answer to everything you know. You don't have to attach or associate everything someone says to directly mean it has something to do with you.

People rarely speak to you anyway. Most of the time they're talking aloud to themselves, which seems to them and to you, that they're talking to you, but they're not, can you see that?

NANCY: No.

JOSEPH: When I say, "You make me angry?" What
I am saying is akin to, "You make me a sweater. You
make me booties. You make me dinner." How can you
make, as in "to prepare" me anything which has to do
with the innermost workings of my brain?
You cannot get in there and move around the circuitry.
Only I can. I can make myself angry about what you
said or failed to say to me. Do you see that now? Do
you see the insanity, as Charley would put it, of how
that works?
          Lysa, why did you get up and clean Satori's
computer in the middle of my speaking?

ANGIE: Because she's uncomfortable listening to
you. She's uncomfortable with what you're saying.
People clean when they're uncomfortable.

BEAU: Then I was never uncomfortable in life
because my room was always a mess.

JOSEPH: Always? As in, never ever clean?

BEAU: Okay, well most of the time it was a mess. On Mondays, Wednesdays, and alternate Sundays you freakin' linguistic perfectionist!!

CHARLEY: All right! You've lost your speaking privileges Joseph. Step aside! Fly aside! Get the heck out of my way. Lysa, you are speaking to us. Do you get the importance of what I am saying? You are speaking to the only people in the world who can give those goddamn doctors a clue as to how, when, where, and why we died.

     They are spending all of their money, your money, the donors and governments money, seeking to find an answer, a cure, or clue to why a 12-year-old would put a bullet to his head as Beau did, or hang themselves as Angie did, or jump from a fucking freeway overpass as I did.

     They think the answers are in a laboratory and we are the rats. Yet how can they study someone that is no longer there? We are dead.

     There are survivors; those who attempted to take their lives and failed.

     Ask them why they attempted to die?

     What did they think death would bring them that life had not?

     What did they need to desire to survive?

No, not just survive, but to be alive, truly alive? What were their actions, their attempts at suicide, saying that their voices could not?

What was most important for their parents and loved ones to know about who they were, about what made them laugh and what made them cry? What was the one thing, that if someone had done, would have given them a reason to live?

Lysa, there are no victims out there. Although I know lots of people who would win an Academy Award for the best portrayal of one, you each have a choice in how you live your life, in how you perceive others words and make meaning of your world, including the world of what happens to you, around you, in you, and outside of you.

You have this mission in life, yes?

Yes.

You have a mission that was created especially for you. I had one. Joseph, Beau, Angie, and Nancy, we all had a mission that was ours and only ours, to fulfill. We failed that mission by cutting our lives short.

Don't you see, we cannot get out of what is ours to fulfill. Now we have the double task of finishing our mission through someone on earth and of learning the lessons we thought we had left behind. It's an illusion, an idea made in the mind of man, to think that he or she knows what death will bring.

How do you know death is not more painful than life? You don't. You just think it's a way out of your problems.

The only way out is through.

The only way through is through.

What is the purpose of my life Charley?

Need you ask that, foolish soul? Not foolish as in stupid, foolish as in asking something of which you already know the answer.

Humans do that too often; ask questions to which the answers they already know. It's as if when the answer comes from outside of them and they can hear that which they already know being said, they tend to believe it more.

This looking for agreement thing has got to be stopped. The other guy always knows better, right?

JOSEPH: Especially if he's got a degree.

ANGIE: Or she.

CHARLEY: Just to let you know, I didn't kill myself because I was left alone. I killed myself because they would not allow me to be. Be as in, just be me; to think as I did, see what I saw, feel as I felt, experience my own version of reality, express myself in my own unique ways.

They didn't feel okay with that.

Locking me up was the doctors and my parent's version of helping me. I was a danger to myself, that's what they told me. "No," I say! I was in danger of losing myself. That's why I chose to die.

You see, humans, you included, think they can stop someone from doing something, namely killing themselves.

People think they can stop someone from doing something and this is a fallacy.

We only know we stopped someone when the result is, they did not do what we stopped them from doing. We intervened when they wanted to die and now they're not dead and we take credit for stopping them from dying.

We actually think that they're not dead because we stopped them from killing themselves.

No, no, no, no, no! This is the biggest lie in the land of effervescent lies.

We cannot stop a person from doing anything just as we cannot stop the sun from rising, the clouds from parting, the moon from shining, the water from falling, the snowflakes from forming, a baby from being born, a baby from choosing to die.

I know what you're thinking—abortion, right? We can stop a baby from being born if a woman has an abortion, right? Wrong! An abortion stops a particular body from coming into existence, being created in that particular period of time, but it does not stop a soul on its way to earth from taking the body of another form.

The soul is destined before it is born to ride a particular course of life. Whose course it is does not matter. Just as if you do the Boston marathon or the New York City marathon, which one you do does not matter if your goal is to run 26 miles. Which particular 26 miles you do is of no significance because the course is the same. <u>The outcome is the same</u>! Only the place and time you do it in is different.

Your home is quite peaceful now. No music, just the tapping of your fingers against the keys. I'm proud of you Lysa. Some people are not comfortable with that level of silence. It is soothing to the soul... our soul and yours.

So we cannot stop people from killing themselves?

This is a difficult concept for you to grasp so I will explain it in the most primitive of ways. The only way you know if you've stopped something is that it stops, right?

So the only way you'll know if you stopped someone from killing themselves, is if they live, right?

Right.

My question to you is, how do you know that what you did stopped them from killing themselves or if what you did gave them a new reason to live and this is why they choose not, not to die, but to live instead.

What you're saying is just the opposite; that the flip side of not killing yourself is that you live.

It goes deeper than that Lysa. You can choose not to kill yourself and still be dead—the walking dead I call it.

You live so that others will not fear your death. You live so that others will not have to feel the pain of you being dead. You live so that others can say they saved you. You live, but not really. Your limbs are moving but inside you feel dead.

Are you saying we should just let you kill yourself? Stay out of the way?

No, no, no! I'm saying if you desire us to live, then help us by giving us a strong enough reason for why we should live.

Don't keep us alive instead, just so you don't have to mourn our death. Instead assist us in finding our reason, our life purpose for being alive.

This is why I chose you, Lysa, for this very task. I knew you would feel passionate enough. You and Satori both have the means to impact the world; the world of those who are living and the world of those who are the living dead.

How?

CHARLEY: I'm so glad you asked. You know, not many people ask how these days. They ask why a lot. "Why me? Why do I always get stuck with these shitty men or bitchy women? Why, why, why?

We make it all up anyhow. Why do I have a headache? Because I didn't sleep much last night or I had that salami sandwich with the white bread. No, it could be the fact that you've been mentally bitching to yourself all day and your head just wants a break from all the chatter.

How do we ever know which is the 'real' answer to the question of why? We don't. We make it all up anyhow. So why don't we make it up good? We always make up the shittiest answers to our heartfelt questions, don't we? Why didn't he call me? I must not be pretty enough.

No, how about because he didn't call. He didn't call because his fingers chose not to dial the phone. Period. End of story.

Now the question is, do you want to go out with a guy who doesn't call when he says he's going to call? Now that's a different conversation. That's a conversation about possibility and choice, not silly answers to meaningless questions.

If the answer to the question why was enough to satiate the ever-so-inquisitive chatterboxes of this world, there would be a lack of chatter in the world right now.

As it stands, millions still pay their therapists in search of the answer to the infamously stupid question, "Why am I so screwed up?"

Ask and ye shall receive. Ask a better question. Get a better answer. How can I be happier? More fulfilled? Find my life's purpose. Now we're talking interesting questions.

And by the way, just for the record, I never asked these myself when I was alive. I asked the stupid ones. But now that I know better, I am doing better. That's real knowledge you know, doing... putting into action what you know, not just knowing for the sake of knowing.

That's just information collecting, which I hear is quite popular down there these days.

November 8, 1999

Is it true that you suffer when we suffer?

ALEXY (age 20): Yes. We suffer when you do, but not in the same way. We don't feel actual pain, like physical pain, we just find it difficult to move on when you're in pain.

It's like if a child is crying and you reach out to help them, but you're behind a wall, so they do not see you there. You're knocking and yelling real loud, but they cannot hear you.

How do you just walk away from that?

The answer is, you don't. But in staying beside you as you grieve for many years, we are putting off the growth of our souls. We have things to do up here as well. So the best thing you can do to assist us in getting to where we need to go is by you moving forward, not like in forgetting about what happened, but in moving forward with what happened so we can do so as well.

One of the things with suicide is that we have to pay the price for our faulty deed. We have broken our agreement.

We have not been faithful to our word and must be punished, not punished in the way you know punished to be, punished as in feeling and seeing the consequences of our actions and the impact those actions had on those still living.

There are no shortcuts Lysa.

We cannot take our lives away just as we cannot create our own lives without the help of two others. Nothing we do we do alone.

Every action, including a failure to take action, has an impact on the world. Nothing we do affects only us. We impact others with our words, our deeds, our moods, and actions.

So in choosing to kill ourselves, we made a choice that MUST be rectified. This means that we can either choose a soul still on earth who is willing for us to assist them in completing their mission or we must assist the souls of the many who are in pain.

I want you to know that just because I no longer have a body in which to deal with my pain doesn't mean I am without my pain. I still have to deal with why I CHOSE TO END MY LIFE.

The problems didn't just go away when I died.
My body did.
My problems did not.
Now I must deal with them from another realm, without the support and love of my family on earth. This has been hard for me, as it is for all suicides, to accept.

It is difficult for us to watch those on earth hurting themselves in the way we once did. We watch you. We watch you ever so closely and we see. We see what you do, what you fail to do and hear what you say or refuse to say...

On Thanksgiving, I watched my mom stuff her face with fried chicken, turkey wings, stuffing, cranberry sauce, and pumpkin pie and then complain, she actually had the nerve to complain, about feeling sick the next day. The food was to blame, she said, as if she had nothing to do with shoving it in her mouth!

I'm sorry if I'm bitching, it's just that I feel so angry when I see all of this pain, pain I used to be a part of, that now I can't do anything to stop. Do you understand the frustration in that?

I thought I would die, go to heaven, become an angel, and that would be that—my life of utter perfection would be complete. But it's not like that for those of us who choose to die -- deliberately, forcefully, with no thought of whom we are hurting.

I was selfish, self-centered and completely egotistical. Do you know how unbelievably egotistical one has to be to take their own life? To you it looks like we hate ourselves; that we think our lives don't matter. But no, this is the big fallacy amongst us suicidiots.

What was our life about when we were there?

Ourselves.

Why didn't we get ours? Why were we doomed to so much pain? We focused on what mommy and daddy and society and our girlfriends or boyfriends or kids or bosses or whatever bogus excuse we could blame for our pitiful state as being the cause, not the effect, of our desire to die. We didn't think of you, the people who were doing everything they knew how to do in an attempt to save us, to make us well.

What about your pain? Wasn't it real for you? You sound so harsh toward yourself.

It's about time I'm harsh. Down there, it looked like I hated myself, but think about it. If someone hates someone or something, do they spend so much time thinking about it? If you hate dogs, do you hang out with them?

No.

If I hated myself, would I have spent so much time with myself, alone in my room? If I'd hated myself, would I have attended all those therapy sessions, talking about no one, but me?

I don't think I hated myself. I think I didn't know how to love myself, which is quite different from hating myself.

CHARLEY: I need to cut in, Alexy. I need to say something about all those doctors who are searching for answers inside a pill. They look into the lab, instead of into our eyes.

They search for answers in something that cannot provide them with what they want

Pills don't kill themselves.

People do.

Pills cannot save us.

People can.

If I was to run in front of a bus, would a pill pull me out of the way or would a person be more likely to do so?

It is this generation of denial, this avoidance of intimacy at all costs, which is killing us. Every living being has been blessed with a heart filled with so much love it could heal the rapturous overture of a wild ocean, stop the monsoon from hitting a small town, and heal a bay filled with garbage and insects.

I'm speaking for all of us when I say that we feel so much pain in doing what we did. <u>We died</u>. We left behind the most precious gift that can ever be given. Not our bodies. Not our jobs. Not even our parents, friends, families, or loved ones.

We left behind the chance to make a difference in a world that will go on without us; a world that is now missing something because we are not there. The world lost many precious souls. They lost the chance to hear our voices speak the words that only we have the power to speak. But now, through you, God bless-sed you, we have been given another chance to have our words be heard.

We will not let you down Lysa. We will speak all the words our hearts long to say. We will guide all those lost souls who think they can find reverence and comfort in heaven and we will teach them to find reverence and comfort on earth.

JEFFREY (age 51): Hello Lysa, my name is Jeffrey Owens. I'm asking that you leave my full name here. God knows I need the publicity. I used to be in the entertainment business. I used to say that business is what killed me. I now know that nothing outside of myself was the cause of my death. I caused my death.

I used to think my life was a dress rehearsal. You know, getting ready for the real thing. When I died, I realized that this was it. The life I had led was the real thing. Not some dress rehearsal for someday.

I was one of those people who used to live for someday. You know, someday I will settle down, buy myself that car I've always wanted, have kids, be happy, but not now. Now I'm too busy gathering all the things that I will 'someday' enjoy.

Boy, did I sure miss the boat. Life is right now. Everything that is happening to you is happening to you right now. The sad thing is that most of us aren't present enough to see it, feel it, enjoy, and relish in the gift that is our lives.

The present. Pre Sent. I now believe we are all Pre Sent to earth with everything we need located conveniently inside our souls. We are sent with all we need in order to do, be, experience, and live the lives we have dreamed.

I have come to learn that the things that make us most happy; the things that make our hearts sing are the very things in which we are supposed to spend our lives doing. Singing, writing, being a lawyer, a doctor, a painter, a carpenter, a designer, an actor, a musician, or whatever we feel most in love with doing, is the very thing we are meant to do. So why don't we do it? Why don't we do the things that bring us great joy?

We're afraid.

We give up.

We don't get the agent, the applause, the money, the prestige, and so we give up doing the very thing that will bring us inner happiness and peace.

And then we blame. We blame our mothers, our father, teachers, girlfriends, boyfriends or whomever told us that we should stop doing the thing we loved and get a real job. We end up blaming them. But you see, this is the lie. There is no one to blame.

Once you get past the age of twelve, you realize that your decisions about what people have told you are just that – your decisions. How can you go through life blaming your low self-esteem on a parent who said you were stupid at age four or a teacher who deemed you would never amount to anything? Yes, they said these words, but it was YOU who chose to believe them. Do you believe everything people tell you? Of course not, so why believe the things that do not bring you joy?

"But maybe they're right," I used to tell myself. There is no right. I could have been right if I had chosen to live and pursue my dreams. I could have proved them wrong. But I didn't. Instead I chose to cop out.

I was afraid of telling the truth; the truth about how much my art really mattered to me. Yes, I was an artist, an agent first and an artist second. That's where the screw up occurred. I had my priorities reversed. I was terrified to admit how much I loved art. The way my paintbrush swirled around the silky colors and made its way onto the virgin canvas, yearning for me to take it in and create something I could call my own.

I was afraid of my passion, my investment in something that meant so much to me. What if I failed? What if no one liked my work? I now know that failure is only a word. I now know that the only way to fail is to quit.

I failed because I quit.

I quit my art and my life. I did not fail because nobody bought my paintings. I did not fail because of anything anyone had said.

I failed because I quit doing the one thing that brought me the most joy; the one thing I could have left to this world, contributed to this universe.

Who was I to make that decision? I now know that decision was not up to me to make.

You cannot leave your dreams behind.

They don't leave you alone.

It's like the guitarist who puts away their guitar, expecting to lose their passion for playing. But then one day, they pick it up, and there it is – the passion. It never leaves you. You can ignore it, drink, smoke, eat, or try to distract it away, but it will not go. Your passion is a monkey on your back that only needs you to acknowledge, nurture, and allow it to become all that it and you are capable of being….

Everything.

It is only when we accept all of who we are, and everything we think we are not, that we can be free. How many of us thought we were free when really, we were not.

It's time to make your case, stake your claim, and ask for what is rightfully yours. This is your time to be bold, audacious, and fearless in your identity. To show, tell, speak, and elaborate upon who you are and what you stand for.

Never mind what they, the people, think or say. You will lift them into a realm unknown to common man; a realm of extraordinary possibility where your shirt hangs out and your boots don't match and you just don't give a damn about either, because it doesn't really matter.

I used to feel afraid when talking to certain people. Do you think that's how doctors felt when they were around you? Afraid?

No, I think we use fear as an excuse to get out of doing what we know is the right thing to do. All of this attention on wondering what others will think, really drains our souls, takes us out of ourselves and into another realm of being—the land of make-believe, where all is pretending and everyone is fearful of being found out.

I think we expect so much from ourselves. We expect to feel no fear when going into an unknown situation and balk at fear once it hits us in the face. We expect fear to be gone at all times, under all circumstances, and if it isn't, we use the presence of fear as an excuse for not going forward with what we know is the highest choice for our lives.

ANGIE: The one thing I still wrestle with is that I wasn't more of who I really am while I was still on earth. I spent so much time, money, and energy thinking up ways to be different than I was. I'd do my hair differently or my nails or wear different clothing and when the lure of that ran out, I would sit on my ass and do nothing.

I think I've been a part of every "crowd" in school. I was a greaser, a jock, a smarty, and a stuck-up bitch. I was the rich girl, the poor waif, the helpless lad, the distressed damsel, and all the while when I was fitting into a particular group, I never stopped to ask myself which of the me's was the real me.

KIMBERLY: Lysa, I want to say something. Okay. This is going to be hard for me to say.

There I go again, planning beforehand that something is going to be hard. Whenever I do that, it always is. It's like I'm psychic or something. I can foretell the destiny of my future. The question is, "Why do I always foretell it bad?"

Anyway, I know you are feeling overwhelmed right now because of the messy web of feelings shot to you from above. But please do not stop. In the end, there will be a clearing, a new beginning from which you will start.

It's as if you are the clean canvas and we are the paint. We will mess you up something awful with our array of clashing colors, but in the end, you will be left with a beautiful portrait painted from the voices above. A portrait you helped paint with your patience and time and your love.

Thank you.

GARY (age 27):   When I was sixteen, I wanted to buy myself a bicycle. But not just any bicycle—a brand new top-of-the-line Schwinn. It cost 500 dollars and all I had was three. I begged my parents to loan me the extra two hundred and promised to pay them within two months time.

I wanted this bicycle so much. I would ride it in my sleep, mount it when awake, and take it on the journeys to far off lands.

I was going to be a world class cyclist and I knew, God did I know, that in order to be that way, I had to become it now. I had to think, act, train, and discipline myself like a world-class cyclist, not when I became one, but in order to become one.

Purchasing the bike was my first step.

My parents refused to lend me the money and refused, even if I came up with the money myself, to allow me to purchase the bike.

"Get a used one," my father said. "Don't waste your money on such nonsense as a new bike. It's not worth it."

You know what I took from that conversation? I'm not worth it.

The denial of being allowed to purchase an item that meant much, crushed every dream I allowed myself to have. The bicycle was not just a bicycle to me. It was ME. And with the denial of it, I threw out my idea that I could ever be or ever achieve what my heart once knew I could.

I resigned.

My parents saw it as me waking up; waking up to reality… a reality in which I no longer desired to live.

When did you decide to die?

When I saw Johnny Scaraponi riding the bike, my bike and saw him take first place for winning the local race. When I saw him kissing Lucille Bagnaponch on the lips after receiving his trophy.

I went home, locked the door, and cried. I bawled louder than a baby, then stopped when I heard footsteps coming up the stairs. Crying wasn't cool with my dad. Crying was a sign of weakness. So I turned off the tears and turned off my heart and sat in my room, lost, alone, in a world of self-pity, denial, and apathy toward life.

It was over for me.

I was sixteen years old and it was over. I'd had enough of this thing... this pain in the ass thing... called my life.

Who was it that walked up the stairs?

My father. He couldn't handle my pain. It reminded him too much of his own. He was in denial of his childhood wounds. I hate to even say that because I now know that our souls cannot be wounded.

What do you mean?

We think our souls are so fragile and dainty, that they'll shatter with too much pain.

This is false.

Our souls are born whole and complete, live whole and complete, and remain whole and complete throughout our lives.

Yes, we feel pain during our lifetimes, some more than others, some more tragic than the next. Yet our souls cannot be permanently wounded.

We are not broken.

You are not broken.

Who you are is and will forever be – whole and complete.

CHARLEY: How about starting from that point? Boy would that wipe out years of therapy.

GARY: That's right. No more poor, broken child, wailing for what you had thought you'd lost. If you knew you were, are, whole and complete, how much could you accomplish in your lifetime?

I'm not saying you won't have to face and deal with things that have hurt you in the past. I'm saying that you won't have to start from the point that you are broken because of something someone did or said to you in the past. They did what they did. They said what they said. And who you are is still whole and complete. Cool, huh?

Very cool.

You see, doctors cannot fix that which is not broken. WE ARE NOT BROKEN. Human beings cannot break. We can feel sad, angry, tormented, uplifted, intrigued, adventurous, hopeful, enthusiastic, alone, lonely, together, connected, and so on.

But we cannot be broken, and that is why, we cannot be fixed.

Doing this feels very strange, like I am not sure if what I am doing is talking to different parts of myself, just like when I wrote Journey From Within and spoke to each character, writing their words through me on the computer screen. How do I know I'm not just making this stuff up?

JOSEPH: How do you know?

That is what I'm asking you. How do I know?

BEAU: You don't know. You never know. Nothing is ever known. You know?

No.

CHARLEY: Lysa, please put aside your need of knowing right now. It's getting in the way of you finding out what you need to know.

We all know more than we think we know. This is your problem, or rather opportunity.

You know so much that you hide what you know because you don't want people to know that you know because knowing would mean or might mean, you know something they don't and that would mean they didn't know that they didn't know that which you knew.

The English version please.

Quit hiding what you know, Lysa. It doesn't look good for your resumé to say, "No one knew how much she knew."

That's the difference between heaven and earth. We can't hide anything up here, nor would we want to.

You won't want to hide when you experience the value of being truly authentic in the presence of another, in the presence of someone who just allows you to be. It's an awesome feeling, one I did not allow myself to experience very often whilst on earth.

I am sure people loved and accepted me, but I didn't allow myself to just be with their love.

I got caught up in the system of…

Gotta do.

Gotta be.

Gotta be somebody.

Gotta do something to be something to have something so I have something to show for being here. I didn't realize that I'd already had the most awesome thing to show for being here – ME. I had me and I… was… enough.

I'm sitting here with Kurt Cobain's suicide note. What does it mean to you when someone who was somebody, according to the world of what is required to be somebody is, kills themselves?

JOSEPH: May I answer this one Charley?

CHARLEY: Joey, go right ahead.

JOSEPH: Being a psychologist when I was alive gave me access to celebrities. I was invited into a world in which they shared with few. What I learned from one celebrity in particular was that life on the outside was not an indicator of life on the inside. If people would just get the power of that statement they'd be way ahead of the game. Life on the outside is not an indicator of life on the inside.

What this means is that our insides are made up of our thoughts, feelings, and beliefs, which often come from our parents, friends, teachers, and even society's ideas about what is appropriate for us to think, feel, and believe.

Half of the stuff you think and believe didn't even originate in you. It's stuff you are fed, handed down, told to feel, think, and believe. Some of us rebel. Some of us agree. But whatever we choose to do, we must remember that no one forces us to believe in something.

We alone must take personal responsibility for what we choose to believe and for the impact those beliefs have on the quality of our world.

I've heard my family members ask why. Why did I die? Why didn't I call them on Sunday when I was supposed to? Why did I instead choose to take my own life? Don't they know I didn't call because if I had, I wouldn't have ended my life?

If I had connected with them, with the love and light that was surrounding me, is always surrounding us, then I wouldn't have had the desire to sit in my darkness and cry.

In order to kill yourself, you must block out all that is good and worthwhile about living and only focus on that which you hate, cannot stand, don't want anymore of.

You cannot be connected to the beauty of life and choose to die.

It doesn't work that way. Just as you cannot be connected to the beauty of another and hate them at the same time. Lightness and darkness do not coexist. One overrides the other at all times. The moment I turn on the light, the darkness is gone. The moment I turn it off, the light does not remain.

It's all a matter of focus, of finding those things that bring light into our lives. They're always there. Life is forever handing you a million miracles, a million reasons to feel happy, but we often deny that beauty and instead, choose to reflect on what is not working in our lives, what is not beautiful, precious, and loved.

There isn't a total resting place where our souls can stop — stop learning, stop seeking, stop enjoying, stop feeling, stop growing, stop dying, stop living… There is no resting place in the land we call faith. People think when they have faith they have to do nothing.

They, I, used to think that I could do nothing, just pray and wait for God to answer my prayers.

Don't you know that if you leave a Buddha at the top of a mountain and come back for him the next day, if he didn't move, he'll still be there? He'll probably have a sore ass, but he'll still be there. Don't you know that if you leave your socks in the middle of the room and no one picks them up, they will still be in the middle of the room when you came home?

What I'm saying may sound trite and basic, but it really comes down to responsibility, for our thoughts, our actions, our words, and our lives. Why did I think my parents and teachers and society owed me a living and a life because of the mere fact that I was alive? I was a spoiled brat in life!

CHARLEY: And you ain't changed a bit in death!

JOSEPH: You see, I can laugh at that today. I can understand that Charley is joking.

CHARLEY. What he doesn't know can't hurt him.

JOSEPH: I'm serious. This is the kind of stuff that would piss me off when I was alive. If anyone would say what I perceived to be the slightest insult, I would freak out. Even if they didn't mean to be rude, I would always find hidden meanings in their words, anything to prove I was a piece of shit. I was looking all over for references to validate my perception of myself as being a piece of shit.

That's why I laugh when I hear people down there complaining they cannot find someone to love. It's such a joke to me that they cannot see what I could not see; that the human race is designed to work for us in whatever means we assign to it.

If I tell my mind I am a piece of shit, my mind will look outside of myself for all the areas that can validate my piece-of-shitness in the world.

Then, of course, I wouldn't be attracted to a woman who saw me better than I saw myself because that would go against everything I thought to be true about me. That would challenge the beliefs I held about myself. And I wasn't going to risk losing my shitty, low self-esteem. No way. Not even for love.

November 8, 1999 — 4:00 p.m.

I am back and I am feeling so very anxious and pissed off. What is it? What is going on with me?

NANCY: It's the emotional flooding of someone who loves. You desire so much to make a difference in the world and are bogged down having to do everything yourself.

You and Satori depend way too much on each other to get the job done. You must reach out to others who can help you lighten the load. You must allow yourselves to go with the flow of life rather than constantly pushing against the tide.

What does that mean? Pushing against the tide?

ANGIE: There you go again, asking questions where questions are not to be asked. What she means is if you constantly demand so much of yourself so that every moment, every mila-second of your day has to be accounted for, then you will surely burst with anxiety and fear.

It is not up to you what you do each day because you are driven by a force beyond your control, driven by a mission where the miniscule and the mundane cannot be accounted for. You are driven to make a masterpiece of your life and doing things like transcribing your friend's poetry book or making fancy brochures, just won't cut it for you.

Listen to your heart, Lysa.

Listen to what it needs to say and then follow it. Diligently. Passionately. Until you arrive at the place in which you desire to be.

The anger and irritability you feel comes from a lack of trust held deep within. You and Satori have been on this roller coaster ride of ups and downs for many years now. Not ups and downs within your relationship, but within your missions in life. There came a time when you both knew what needed to be accomplished and you could ensure that your mission progressed.

But the one thing you forget to solidify in your mission was the virtue, the inner virtue of trust. Trust in that which could not be readily seen. Trust in the oasis of love that you have called your home. Trust in the creator called life. Trust in your soul who knows exactly what to do.

How can you trust yourself when you have so little faith that your passions and gifts will be fully realized? How can you rest in the knowing that who you are and what you have to contribute to the world, is important and immense?

You must stop and stand in the light of your being; knowing that all is well within your garden, taking time to enjoy the fruits of your labor each and every day.

Trust from the innermost recess of your soul that you are cared for, taken care of, looked after, and well. Trust that the purpose of your life is that which brings you the most joy.

Ask not what your next move shall be. Ask not what you shall <u>do</u>. Instead, be calm and quiet and one with the force of life that has created you, that cares for you, and watches over you, from the day you were born, until always.

What is the sickly feeling I used to get inside?

Feelings are there to teach us. They are signals on what needs to be heard. Like the annoying fly whose job it is to teach you patience, the knawing feeling in your gut is there to teach you peace. To be with whatever is going on is the highest gift you can give yourself… and another.

We have such a hard time just being with people, especially when they are in pain. I watched my family grieving for my loss. I watched people around them, trying desperately to stop them from feeling and expressing their pain. It wasn't that they didn't want my parents to cry, it was seeing them cry that made them uncomfortable. <u>They</u> could not deal with the pain. It's like the handicapped child who is fine with her condition, but the parents and teachers who are not. They are uncomfortable being with someone who is handicapped.

So much of your world is about changing, fixing, altering, and adjusting what is, into what we think it should be. Even to allow your spouse to just be, however he is, exactly as he is, is most difficult for you, Lysa. I know this comes from the love you have for him, yet the love you have for him must be extended to include all parts of him; especially those parts which complain.

When he cries like a baby, hold him gently in your arms. When he sings like a Cherokee, join him in verse and song.

When he says, "I don't know what to do," tell him he does. Do not tell him the answers to what is his destiny to find out. You must learn to be with each other, in each other's arms, with the utmost sincerity in knowing that all is well, all is cared for, you are cared for… because you are alive.

Once you learn the importance of a smile, a laugh, a hand held, an encouraging word, a soft caress, a passionate attempt, you will then understand the meaning of life.

The most important aspect of life, at the end of your life, and every day in between, is to love.

Love with all of your heart... and then some. Love until there is no more and watch as the flow of the river catches up and fills you once more. You can never run out of that which is eternal.

Money, as you already know, is a means to an end. Love, compassion, charity, congruence, spirituality, faith, fullness, fun, joy, caring, sorrow, and servitude, these are the emotions of the soul. I ask you one question, Lysa.

What is that?

Whom and what do you love?

I love my family, my husband, and my dog. I love humankind and orchids and freedom to self-express, and discovery and creation.

I love knowledge - applied knowledge and wonderment and not knowing and being okay with not knowing and feeling the lightness of life bellowing upon my skin and fortitude and reverence and peace of mind, and passion and inspiration and smiling and movies and the sun and connecting with others and laughter and life...All of life... I love all of it.

What is the purpose of life itself?

CHARLEY: To love.

ANGIE: To live fully while you are here.

JOSEPH: To get laid. Just kidding.

CHARLEY: No, you're not.

JOSEPH: Arthur told me to say that. He said it would knock you off kilter receiving an unexpected response from me. The purpose of life is to enjoy all that encompasses living.

ARTHUR (age unknown):   To hear your soul sing.

ANGIE: Yeah. I like that.

CHARLEY: Uh oh, they're in love.

Can you fall in love in heaven?

ARTHUR: A better question would be, can you NOT fall in love in heaven? All love is heaven. There is nothing else but love up here.

What about the suffering Charley talked about? The sort of suffering akin to sins, for lack of a better word, wrongdoings, breaking your contract with the universe, what about this?

JOSEPH: People think the only way to suffer is to make yourself or somebody else wrong for what they have done.

Suffering need not be painful. There isn't a painful or not painful connotation attached to it. It's just suffering. I don't know any other way to put it.

At the end of your life, everything is reflected back to you. All the love you have given. All the pain you have caused, yourself and others. You get to re-experience the love AND you get to step into the other's shoes and experience the pain and hurt your actions caused them.

If you really felt what it felt like to hurt another, you wouldn't do it. If you could walk in their shoes for just a moment, you would take back all of the pain you have caused.

That's why there's no punishment from others up here. No damning God to blame us for our sins. We are our own judge and jury. Self-punishment and regret is worse than any punishment from the outside.

So we make ourselves suffer?

JOSEPH: Yes and no. We suffer because we choose suffering thoughts, words, and actions.

Just like what happened a moment ago regarding you and Satori. You commented that you did not enjoy a cord he was playing on the guitar. ONE CORD! And he stopped playing guitar completely. He instead put on a puppy face, pressed his hands against his cheeks, and sat there, waiting for you to relieve him of his self-imposed pain.

We choose everything in our lives; every mood, every disappointment, we choose it all because we know that our needs will get met by doing so. Satori is sitting there, knowing he looks like a sad, ditty puppy. He knows if he holds his face in his hands long enough, you'll stop writing and come to soothe his pain

CHARLEY: All Satori needs right now is to BE, to be with the choices he's made, is making, in this very moment.

Nothing exists between you and Satori except a gust of air and a sweet smelling smile. You are he and he is you, and just as there is nothing you can do to "take away" his pain, there is nothing that needs to be done to take away his pain because there is no pain that needs to be taken.

Nothing is there. Do you see that? Its not like pain exists and you can extrapolate it from the gustoes of his groin. It's not like the pain that you speak of is there, like a corroded artery that needs to be flooded, drained away.

Pain does not exist, except in the realm of words. Words create the experience and make it feel real. Right now, Satori is sitting with his hands over his eyes and his head slightly down and you call that pain. I call it peaceful. How would it be for you if you called it peaceful?

A lie.

Why?

Because the energy emanating from him does not resemble peace. I know when he is in pain.

And that is because you know him from already knowing him. You do not approach him as a man you have not yet met, curious as to why his hands are cupped around his face. You know him, greet him, meet him, with an already knowingness of who you think he is, of who you have made him up to be.

What would happen if right now, you erased your memory of him, if you erased what happened with the guitar and instead, greeted him with a newfound curiosity as to why this man, this good-looking man, is sitting with his hands cupped upon his face.

What would you find out if you got into bed each night without thinking you already knew who he was?

We'd have an even hotter sex life.

You'd have to call the fire department.

Ha Ha.

I am serious. This is why relationships fail, why we get bored with one another and with life. It's because we think we know what everything is.

We do not <u>listen</u> to each other. We already always listen to what they said a week ago, a moment ago, last month, last year, ten years ago.

When was the last time you listened for the first time? Listened in the moment, that moment, to what was actually being said?

When was the last time you listened with freshly cleaned ears? When you saw with clearly cleansed eyes?

When you loved with an unguarded heart?

(I get up and kiss Satori.)

CHARLEY: That was nice. Kissing him. Telling him that you are sorry. Telling him that it was your listening and not his guitar playing, that ticked you off. Just as sometimes you listen to Michael Bolton and love him and other times you are not in the mood for his music, in that moment, the music didn't sit right with you, not him. This is the greatness of who you are Lysa. It is in all of us, in every moment, to begin again, to start anew.

Every moment of life imagine what it would be like if we ate when we were eating. If we made love when we were touching our lover. If when we laughed, we didn't just "laugh," we belly laughed, allowing ourselves to snort, cackle, rupture with joy.

What if we knew that what we had to offer the world was not only okay, but was necessary, needed, required? What if you knew that you mattered and made a difference? What if?

What about all of you missing from the world?

There is nothing missing. There is only that which is no longer there. The universe will go on with you or without you, yet that is not the point, my point. We must realize how small we are in the scheme of things and how big we can possibly be.

You've got to stop waiting for the other guy or gal to do your job, the work which is set out for you to do. Who gets the muscle if I work out at the gym? Me. I do.

Doing is not the essence of life—being is.

What scares you is not so much what others will think of you, but rather, how will you know yourself once you transform yourself to be that which is your essence to be.

How would you know yourself if you did not look as you do? How would you know your essence if all that was inside of you was released? How would you know yourself if your eyes, your nose, your mouth, your "personality" and everything else that is changeable in you, was different? How do you know you are you? How could you tell the difference between day and night if there was no darkness, no lack of light?

How would you tell the time if clocks ceased to exist, and time as you now know it, was not the determinant of when to get hungry, horny, or satisfied, of when to go to sleep, to work, or to play? What would life be like if life, as you have known it until now, suddenly changed?

Wow! We sure went off into a different realm of questioning, a radically different path. And now I would like to get back to...

CHARLEY: Of course you would. You would like to get back to what is safe and familiar.

What is the purpose of this book?

In the world of all worlds, there is only one truth. This truth masquerades as other truths when it's put in different contexts, like in different religions and the like. When you boil down all religious paths, all spirituality, all that every person has ever known to be true, you reach a point of knowing; an intersection where all paths cross.

It is in that intersection where truth and justice and love and carefree living and all that good stuff we spend our lives searching for, resides.

This book is that intersection.

This book is that knowing.

People recognize truth when they come across it.

Why do you think you chose to die?

ANGIE: I wasn't given a reason, didn't find my own reason, to live. If someone like you had come along and shown me, assisted me in finding the way, my way, the one that would lead me back to myself, my true self, I think I would have chosen to live.

That is a big statement. Most likely, it will get your parents upset.

That is not a big task to accomplish, being that they are upset most of the time.

What I'm saying is that I now know what my soul needed in order to find a reason to live.

I hate saying the word alive, because you, your presence, is so alive to me right now.

Thank you. That makes a difference. My life was not designed for me to just "be." Being was a waste of time. I had to do, do, do. Head cheerleader, prettiest girl on the team, boys loved me, most popular, yada, yada, yada.

What I didn't know then is that there is a reason we are called human beings, not human doings. Being is essential to living.

If you cannot be with yourself exactly as you are, not in some future date when you get better, but right here, right now, then how can you do anything worthwhile with your life? And how can you be with another? You cannot.

I learned the hard way how not to be. I would not allow myself to relax, not relax as in lounging on the couch, but relax my mind. The world was going to stop if I didn't do something with my life. And because I didn't feel like I was doing enough, I stopped my life.

November 9, 1999

Good morning my friends! I just want to thank you for giving me this opportunity to serve you. It is a gift and a blessing.

NANCY: Can I talk to you this morning Lysa?

Of course.

I keep so much hidden that no one has a chance to get to know the real me.

I'm a fake.

A fraud.

I hate living this way—hated living this way. Yes. I am dead. I hate that word. It sounds like I was a piece of meat which is now slaughtered, cut up, seasoned, cooked, and served.

What made you realize you were dead?

Charley did. He made me realize I was dead when he showed me my mother and father sitting in the living room of their home. I went there and attempted to speak to them. I stared directly into my father's eyes and he into mine. He did not flinch. He said nothing. But then, he cried. He took a photo of me from beside the couch, held it to his face, and sobbed like a newborn baby.

He was so pathetic that I actually, for the first time in my life, felt sorry for the guy. My mother, usually stoic and reserved, stared at my father for a moment or two and then crawled from the couch onto his lap.

They held each other and sobbed until the early hours of the morning. I felt so helpless, so insignificant. There was nothing I could do to relieve their pain, the pain that I had caused them.

Being in the presence of my parents and not being able to comfort them or relieve their grief made me realize what I had done. I know that it sounds crazy to think that someone can kill themselves and not realize they're dead.

But if people can live in castles and mansions and still feel impoverished and poor, then souls can walk through the pearly gates of heaven and still deny that they're there.

How do you feel now?

Abandoned, alone, afraid, and fearful of what I have done and how it will impact the lives of those I've left behind, namely my daughter, Luchia.

How old is she?

Fourteen.
Dammit!
How can I have been so selfish to have killed myself when she must be thinking that she wasn't worth enough, wasn't a good enough reason for me to live. She wasn't enough of a purpose for me to continue my life.

Is that true?

No. Of course not! How dare you! I'm sorry. I just feel so freggin' guilty over all of this. I don't know how I will cope for the next gazillion years or however long of a time I will be here. I cannot watch her down there, struggling for the rest of her life because mommy didn't know how to cope. Poor, poor mommy, that was the story of my precious daughter's life. I was so damn selfish!

CHARLEY: Was?

NANCY: Get out of here Charley!

CHARLEY: You're funny Nan, you still think you can order me out of here like you did to Luchia. You think I'll leave without putting up a fight, like she did. Well, let me let you in on rule number one of Heaven. I can leave and still be here. There ain't no place to hide out in heaven.

What would hiding out give you?

NANCY: Safety. Security. The illusion of being in control. If no one can get to me, no one can hurt me.

CHARLEY: Or love you.

NANCY: I don't think many people would be banging down the door to do that.

CHARLEY: I would.

NANCY: Yeah right. I used to hide out in Supermarkets and at home, pretending when my friends rang the doorbell that I was not there. I used to hide out at work, in the corridor between my office and the bathroom.

Sometimes I would hide out in the bathroom stalls, waiting until all the feet were out before I washed my hands and raced back to my office.

Did hiding out ever give you what you wanted?

NANCY: No. That's the big joke, or heartache depending on how you look at it. I felt more alone, afraid, abandoned, and disillusioned each time I hid out. Can you turn the music lower?

Of course.

Thank you. I love those words, "of course." They sound so eloquent and delightful. In my lifetime, I have made many requests and until you, I have never heard the words "of course" as a response to one of my requests.

CHARLEY: Maybe because what you made were demands, not requests. Maybe, and I say this with all sincerity Nancy so don't get defensive, but just maybe you didn't, until now, even know what a request was and so you didn't get the response of "of course." Could that be possible?

NANCY: Anything is possible Charley.

CHARLEY: Great attitude.

NANCY: A bit too late, don't you think?

Why do you think most people commit suicide?

CHARLEY: Feeling hopeless.

What causes someone to feel hopeless?

CHARLEY: Lack of hope.

Thank you Charley. Next...

CHARLEY: I don't know 'the' answer. I only know 'my' answer, which is that I felt hopeless when I saw the world the way it was, with all the harsh attitudes, intolerances, and pain.

You see, my parents refused to believe that I was okay. They believed the doctors instead of me. The doctors swore I was manic-depressive and bi-polar and depressed. They didn't know what to do with me so they locked me up.

And it was there, within the confines of America's finest nuthouse, that I lost all hope.

What made you lose all hope?

CHARLEY: Everything! Every single thing. The way the nurses glared at me. The way they assessed every nuance of my being as if it were a crack needing repair. The way the doctors called my name like I had done something wrong.

I got hospitalized more times before the age of twenty-one than I got laid…. and I got laid a lot!!

I told them that I saw the world from a different floor. They didn't see what I saw because they weren't looking through the same window. They refused to come to my floor and admire my view. They wanted me to go where they lived, to where they felt comfortable. Screw that! I wanted to stay where I chose to reside.

We call people crazy for not seeing as we do. But who's really crazy? Is it I, for not seeing what they did or they for not seeing as I?

I feel stuck this morning. The words aren't flowing.

CHARLEY: It's not the words that are not flowing, Lysa. It's you. I'm all flow. I'm ready to go.

What do I do?

Grow up. You were like a little baby this morning. Satori told you to get out of bed so he and you could connect. But no, you stayed in bed. You would not budge because no one is going to tell Ms. Lysa Mateu when it's time to get up.

You're like a little baby, saying no just because mommy or daddy said yes. Staying in bed just because Satori said for you to get up.

That used to be my biggest game—defying the odds. Defying in general. Whatever society said, I said the opposite. It was my poor way of feeling like I had some control over my life, over myself.

How do I stop doing that?

You stop doing that.

How?

Exactly.

How Charley? How do I stop staying up so late?

You turn off that little button on the side of
your computer, the one to the left of your keyboard.
You shut it off before he hits the bed, then you nuzzle
your neck in close to his, and whisper sweet, sexy,
organically orgasmic words into his ear, then have sex if
you like, or not, or just cuddle.

You make it sound so easy.

It is.

I always knew you were brilliant.

I knew that too, that was the problem. I KNEW I was
brilliant, but I didn't DO anything about being

brilliant. Knowing isn't enough, in case you haven't mastered that one.

Have I not?

No. You know so much Lysa. You know to call those agents about your movie. You know to make appointments with producers, directors, agents, and the like, yet you do not, or rather, you hesitate doing the very thing that will bring you joy.

Why?

CHARLEY: BECAUSE… This is the stupidity of why. For example, we are 'dead' and doctors are attempting to come up with the reason as to why we took our own lives. They are looking in the wrong place. I can make up a reason, one that sounds particularly logical, as to why I took my own life, and you know what, it won't be the truth because someone, somewhere out there, was going through the same exact problems as I and did not choose to kill himself. Some got through their pain without taking their life.

Until now, everyone has been researching and searching for the answer to why, and…

They've been wasting your time.

Who?

The doctors. You've been researching what the doctors
have been doing in an attempt to understand their side.
Big waste of your time. The answers lay in what you
and Satori will bring to the table of recovery and life-
enhancement, not in what the doctors have already
been doing. Are people still killing themselves?

Yes.

The truth is that no one can come up with the all-time,
sure thing, cure to obliterating suicide from the face of
the earth.

Oh yeah, just watch me.

Big girl with big dreams.

Anything is possible. Isn't that what you said?

Yes, but… If we told you what was really possible in the course of your lifetime, there would be no fun in finding this out for yourself.

Why have my hands been cold and clammy, sweating one moment and freezing the next, since the time I was seven?

JOSEPH: Souls were trying to alert you. They had something to say.

I should have responded.

Did you?

I should have.

There is no <u>should have</u> in heaven. It's a rhetorical question to ask if you should have done something, as if answering it will automatically cause you to go back in time and do things differently.

It would be great if we could rewind life. Do it over.

You can, next time around.
But for now you must be responsible.

92

Responsible for what you think, say, do, and not do. We are forever imprinting the world with our thoughts, visions, and actions.

You know, if you visualize hurting a person, then an imprint of your hatred goes out to them and they immediately feel the effects of your crime. It is a crime to hate. It is a crime to think hate. There is no difference.

Surely there is a difference between hurting someone in your mind and hurting them in real life.

What is real life? Please explain this to me.

You know what I mean.

No, I don't. People talk about life as if there's a "real" life and a "fake" life. The one we relate to is the fake life. Like the actor working as a waiter, refusing to acknowledge that his waiter role is not his fake life. It's his real life.

Do you understand what I'm saying?

You people on earth live like there's a better life coming around the corner. Just wait long enough and hang in there and you will get to live the life you've always envisioned.

BULLSHIT!

This is your life right now!

I keep getting these weird feelings about something happening to Satori. I don't want to lose him. Will I?

No.

Will we be together forever?

No.

How come?

Because there is no forever, there is only right now. Anyway, the fears and apprehensions you seem to suffer from lately, they're just a manifestation of what Satori is feeling. You have taken on his fears.

How can I do that? Then I would be blaming him.

So, blame him. He blames you for lots of shit. We all do it – blame one another for everything gone wrong in our lives. We either blame each other or we blame society or the bad guys on T.V. or the media or consumers. We've always got to have something to

94

blame. God forbid we took responsibility for our lives. What would happen then?

We'd be successful.

Hallelujah! It's about time.

For what?

For people to get the picture about how truly responsible for their lives they are. No one can take credit when you write a book except for you, right?

Or you.

No, we are the silent authors. We don't get the residuals. Not even bonus pay.

I'll see what I can do. Hello…

MICHAEL (age 29):   I died when I was at the top of my career. I had money, fame, and success; all of the material stuff, yet it didn't give me…

Happiness?

Love.

How do you know you weren't loved?

MICHAEL: I don't know, not for real. I made it up. I used to drive my wife crazy with my insecurities. I was always trying to prove how unworthy I was. She wouldn't accept it. She always saw the best in me.

I got tired of being with someone who refused to see the truth, at least what I thought was the truth about who I really was.

I now know that my truth was a lie.

November 10, 1999. My birthday. No writing.

November 11, 1999

Hello my friends. I am back and I am passionate about hearing from you today. I just spoke with...

CHARLEY: We know already. We are always with you, listening to every conversation, every word your mouth utters, everything.

I forgot. I'm sorry.

No need to always be sorry. No need to apologize for that which you did not know. Way too many people use I'm sorry as an automatic response rather than a unique way of expressing their genuine sorrow. Just an observation.

Thanks.

Lysa, you came here to fulfill a specific purpose; one that no one else can fulfill. You have been called upon for greatness.

You and Satori are here to make a difference. I was there to make a difference as well. All of us up here, who took our own lives, were. Yet we did not see that as clearly as you see it now. We did not see it at all in fact. We were blind to the brightness of our beauty. We were blind to the magnificence that our souls were meant to reveal. We were alone and lost in our self-pity, self-deceit, and in the believing of those folks who disguise themselves as helpers and healers when in fact they are hurters and deceivers.

I am talking about the drug companies and HMO's and all of the doctors who participate in their harmful charades. Yes, I do believe the intention in scanning the brains of depressed folks and looking for chemical abnormalities was a good one at first.

But once doctors became keen to the amount of money that could be made by doping up the sad and depressed… the weird and the willful, they left the talking, listening, understanding, and discovering, behind.

Look inside any psychiatric ward and you will see the patients telling more to each other than to their doctors. In the night, when all is quiet and foregone, the truth is often revealed as to just how sane these people really are. What I mean by this is, when no one is watching these so-called "sick" folks, they suddenly become normal, as if a white coat and an I.D aggravate their disease.

Joshua, why did you kill yourself?

JOSHUA (age 15):   You're not going to believe this, but I did it, thinking I was cool. I thought it would be cool to end my life; cool to see if I could experience a new life on the other side. Ya know, die just to die.

Is that really why you did it? To die just to die?

No. But it sounds cool, doesn't it?

Not to me.

Are you a prude when it comes to things like these?

What things are you speaking of?

Charley just told me to shut up.

You were fifteen years old Josh! Why?

> So what? Why? Why? Why?
> Why not?
> Why the hell shouldn't I choose to end my life?
> I had nothing to live for. Nothing that juiced my veins
> and made me feel truly alive. Sure, sometimes I felt that
> way, alive, I mean. But it was usually when I smoked
> pot and drank Budweiser.
>
> Then I got afraid I'd turn out like my old man.
> You see, my dad was an alchy and I didn't want to end
> up on the couch next to a buck-toothed old man who
> had nothing but BURP to say to me after school. He
> was a loser and so was my mom for marrying him. I
> wasn't going to end up on that couch. Not me.
>
> I bet you think I'm stupid, but I'm not. I was
> smart when I was alive.

I was so damn smart. I used to ace all of my exams and you know what old pops would say when I came home from school with all A's on my report card?

BURP.

That's what he'd say as he slid my report card under his wet mug of beer.

What is it you wanted from death that you felt you couldn't get from life?

Feelings.

I felt nothing when I was alive and I hoped that death would knock me to my senses and make me feel something more than the dull ache that penetrated my being on a daily basis.

Wait. I guess I just contradicted myself by saying that I did not feel something and then describing to you the dull ache I felt. Okay, I did feel something before I died.

Pain.

All I ever felt was pain.

CHARLEY: That's ALL you ever felt? Come on! Never a hard on for a girl or a woody in the wind?

JOSHUA: No, of course I felt horny… So okay, here I go being a hypocrite again. Okay, I did feel a drop of pleasure mixed in with my pain and sometimes, yes, I even felt aroused and enchanted and all of that goo-goo stuff that goes with falling in love, hence the word 'falling.' How can you ever fall and not get hurt? You cannot, especially with a girl like Gloria. I was so in love with Gloria.

She was the one girl that took my heart out of my head and made me feel like I was magical.
She saw me as the perfect guy.

CHARLEY: And then she got glasses.

JOSHUA: Yeah Charley, you can shut up now.

Gloria was in awe of me. I felt the touch of her fingertips moments before they met my skin. It was the weirdest, strangest, most incredible thing. And then…. it… she… was gone.

And so was I.

My heart and soul… Every bone in my body ached for her. It even hurt to breathe. I was in pain all of the time… never without. Gloria, the memory of her, became my battlefront scar. She became the wound from which I would not heal.

101

It was tragic, so thoroughly tragic, that the only way I knew to get it out of me was to put it to music. So I strummed that sweet lady out of my soul until there was no more of her to be played; until the song of sweet Gloria was silenced forever.

And what happened to Gloria?

She met some other guy, screwed him silly, got pregnant and left town.

Does she know that you died?

Now... she does.
> She's here... with me.
> Got killed in a car crash. Was running across the street with her newborn baby and supposedly, didn't see the four-wheeler speeding her way. She slammed into the front. The baby met the driver on his windshield. They're both here, although the kid has gone to a different part of heaven.

Why? Don't babies go with their mothers?

Not babies whose mothers killed them.

She did?

Yep, she saw it as perfect out for a life she no longer wanted to lead.

Is she there with you?

Nope. Debra is though. Debra is my guide. She was nineteen when she took her own life. But that was centuries ago. She chose to not be reincarnated into a body for another two thousand years. She wanted to stay here and help us—the losers of heaven, as she so affectionately calls us.

November 12, 1999

I feel so nervous now, like the end of my life as I know it, is soon to be over.

JOSEPH: This is good thing, Lysa. One must always leave behind what is familiar in order to be introduced to what is unfamiliar. The unfamiliar may be scary, but it's the stuff that makes us grow.

Does growth have to be painful?

No. Only when we resist growth does it become a painful experience. What you resist – persists. Isn't that the truth?

My truth or the universal truth?

Is there really a difference?

No, but why does living in this world take so much maintenance?

Does it? Or are you just speaking from the mouths of others? Are you just speaking that which you have been taught to believe?

There's just so much to take care of and handle each day. So many papers.

Do you think that if you got rid of all the papers in the world, that the world would not continue to run?

Paper is only necessary because the instrument of understanding, your mind, is not being used at its fullest capacity.

Telepathy.

That's how I'm communicating with you right now, isn't it? And this is how we all can communicate with one another if we so desired.

How?

Practice makes perfect.

I feel like a hypocrite. Promoting all this anti-suicide stuff, these tools for empowerment and better living, when the truth is, I don't know if I like this world so much. I don't know if Satori wasn't around, if I would feel much like living.

This is not because I would want to die, but because this world seems so cold sometimes.

Yes, there is beauty. Yet how much of it actually sustains you? How much of what goes on daily actually sustains and nurtures your soul? There seems to be so much in the way of expressing the truth. The truth about how much people matter to us... to me.

What stops you?

Fear.

Easy answer.

You learned that one in third grade.
Give me another.

Tiredness.

Gosh Lysa, you really did pay attention when your mother spoke to you. Give me an answer that is truly your own.

Is there any such thing?

No, but make believe you've come up with one.

The word that comes to mind is faith. But that doesn't make any sense. Why would faith keep me from expressing my highest self, from loving those whom I hold most dear to my heart?

Why do you think?

You sound like a coach.

I was one in life. Now tell me, why would faith come between you and the full expression of yourself?

Because if I felt faith when I moved toward people and they felt fear, I would be overbearing, too overbearing for them to be around and that would make them want, desire, to leave me.

Is that the truth? Have you experienced people leaving you when you've walked toward them with faith?

No.

So you've made that one up too! You naughty little critter! It's the writer in you. It's the part of you that makes things up. Don't worry. I did it as well.

I used to make up that my mother did not love me and my father thought I was a pain in the ass. I used to make up that I was worthless, untalented, and no good. I used to tell myself these things and believe them. Anything you tell yourself for a long enough period of time becomes the truth, you know.

Is that what got you where you are? Believing in those lies?

Yes and no. Part of what got me here was my believing the lies told to me by others. Those came first. The lies my family told me, and then came the lies I

107

told myself. I didn't know how to direct or control my habitual feelings and thoughts.

I didn't know how to be the master of my mind and the controller of my fate. I was taught that life just happened to you.

It doesn't?

No, it doesn't.
You HAPPEN to life.
Life doesn't just happen to you.

November 14, 1999

I have not been back for several days and I feel somewhat disconnected by this fact. I began doubting what I was accomplishing in having this written through me.

CHARLEY: The spirits spooked you. Isn't that true?

Yes. But sometimes I feel like I forget how to get out of my own way. Like when I was five, ten, or fifteen years old, I knew how to do this… Now, I remember. And then, I forget.

No, you chose not to remember.

There is a difference.

When you choose not to remember, it's your own doing. You consciously choose to not recall that which once gave you pleasure and power. You choose to put aside all that is within your soul and forfeit your right to be bright in exchange for the ever-so-shitty prize of public acknowledgment and admiration from dumbos.

What is a dumbo?

A dumbo is person who refuses to see what is right there in front of them.

How can I convince doctors of what I have seen, heard, and written from you?

CHARLEY: You are not here to convince. You are here to share. You know what I've been wondering about? I've been wondering how all those doctors know if Prozac or Zanax really works?

I mean, does the drug itself change the brain chemistry or does the person's belief that the drug will change the brain chemistry cause the change? Which one is true?

Whichever they believe to be true?

Right-o Lysa! You're catching on to this believing thing. You see, nothing in itself is true. You, me, the people of the world, we make up our minds as to what is true and what is not.

I thought living was painful and death was my escape. I believed that. I thought it was true. But now that my body is gone, I have changed my mind. It wasn't so bad down there.

I would love to go back and do it all over again… differently this time, taking with me all of the knowledge and understanding that this excursion from life has given me.

I have learned that no one is born deficient or defective, even though outward appearances may seem that way.

No human being who has ever walked the earth was born without the inner tools and resources to master their emotions, master their inner drives, and make the outer expression of their lives reveal all that is yearning to be expressed from within.

Then why don't we fully express ourselves?

We do. Just not in front of people.

We express ourselves in the shower, to our dogs, our babies, in the car, bathroom, in the closet when we're getting dressed. We express ourselves when no one is looking.

Why?

Why not? It is safe that way. You cannot get locked up or arrested doing that which no one sees. We have been led to believe there is safety in solitude. But you tell me, is there anything safe about being trapped in a body unwilling to express all that is within?

How cruel would it be to lock up a monkey in a small cage, never allowing him to see the light of day or run, climb, swing, and shout in the jungle in which he was born? How cruel is this? And yet, we do it to ourselves everyday.

We create self-imposed prisons and then look for someone else to find the key.

We hold the key.

What I have learned is this: People will defend what they believe to be true even when an abundance of contrary evidence is revealed. They will discard whatever does not fit into their model of the world just so they can remain true to that which they were taught.

If they were to go against their innate thought systems, those embedded within their consciousness from the earliest years, they would literally be up against not knowing and this scares them. Better stick with what you know, even if it's shit, than venture into unknown territories and risk being the fool.

To not risk is the biggest risk of all. To remain aloof to what you could be is to play the fool in life.

Where is this book going, may I ask?

You just did.

If you were to lighten up and allow us to do the talking, all will be fine. You will get in everything you need to say, but the surest way NOT to do this is to attempt to control or even worse, worry, about that which you fear will not be revealed within the confines of this book. So, in the words of the Almighty God - LIGHTEN UP!

VERTITUDE: My name is <u>Vertitude</u>. I am an angel who was born long before the others and died many deaths throughout their life.

I have answered many questions and will continue to answer that which you seek to have revealed. I only ask one thing from you.

Yes. What is that?

I ask you to trust. Completely trust that which comes through the fingertips from which you write.

Deal.

Good. First question.

What is the purpose of life?

> For each it is different, but for each there is one.
> Many paths.
> One purpose.
> For you it is to heal the souls who have lost connection with their purpose, their path.
> The only way you can do that is to remain connected to your own.
> You cannot teach that which you have not learned, or rather... remembered.
> And you cannot consider having learned that which you do not practice. Not practice as in repeat the action.
> Practice as in, become the action.

Be that which you seek to have expressed and revealed in the world. You cannot see something that is not, has not already been formed in its completion within you. Whatever visions you have seen with clarity in your mind are visions that are in essence, complete.

The Academy Award, the transformation of the educational system, the love between you and Satori, you and your family, you and all people. The cleansing of the earth. The salvation of your soul. All that you have ever seen to be real for you, if only for a moment, has the propensity for becoming real in the world.

Even the bad stuff then?

There is no "bad" stuff. There is only that which you do not think would bring peace or joy. There is nothing out there, in the world, which could harm you, so nothing you have ever envisioned in your mind's eye should be revered as fearful or not desired to be seen or felt.

So whatever we choose to focus on will be our reality and all that stuff?

Yes. And no. What will come to pass is only that which brings you closer to your purpose—your life's mission, if you will. Nothing you have ever done or failed to do has taken you further away from your life's mission, even though appearances may reveal the opposite of what is so.

Nothing, you as a human being in a body can do, is powerful enough to destroy the mission you agreed to fulfill long before you took one step, breathed one breath, on this earth. Nothing stops your mission… <u>not even death.</u>

Why is it so difficult for people to get out of their own way?

Ask me questions about suicide.

Okay. Why suicide? Why do some see it as an option and others see it as a cop out?

Why did you choose to wear a black shirt today and not a gray one?

Why did you choose to stay home and write instead of going out with Satori and your mom?

Why are you hesitating to call back some friends but at ease when responding to others?

Yes, tell me. Why?

You tell me.

Because of the meanings I attach to wearing certain clothes, how I think wearing them will make me feel. How I think calling certain people will make me feel.

Nonsense. That's the psychobabble you learned. Tell me the real reason you choose a black shirt, to call James but not Katherine, to stay home and not go out. Why? Tell me now.

I have no reason. Is that what you desire me to say?

Is it the truth?

Yes… and no. I think there must be a reason.

How do you know?

Because there must be a reason for why I do some things and not others.

What is the reason then? Come on. Make one up. A good one! Tell the others who do not yet know.

Tell them how we humans make our entire lives a story.

Or saga.

Unfortunately, yes. Tell them how we act like damsels in distress, when in reality, we are the directors, writers, and producers of our lives.

How many of us are writing quality movies?

Not many.

We're all waiting for that someday—that day when it's all going to come together. When all the hard work we have put in, finally comes to fruition.

That SOMEDAY is going to be quite a day! I'm looking forward to seeing it.

It's not going to happen, is it? There is no "someday" in the calendar of weeks.

No, but we can make one up if you'd like.
        We, you, can make up the world to be any way you desire it to be.

That's not true. It's not true that people can live or be however they choose.. People lock them up, you know. You act "crazy" and people can lock you up.

Not if you get a couple of people to agree with you, with your point of view. Talking to a tree is only crazy if you're doing it alone. Gather a group of people to join in and you've got an acceptable form of group therapy. Sanity in numbers, isn't that what they say?

Who?

They. What are "they" going to think? What will "they" say? Lets check with them, the experts and get "their" opinion.

How can I best express what I have learned?

BY EXPRESSING IT.

How can I reveal the notions that ring true in my mind, in the minds of all those who have been abused, used, made wrong, and forgotten, all in the name of psychiatry and science. How can I unleash the pent up storehouse of my mind and let it flow in a coherent,

understandable manner so that people will get exactly
what I desire to say.

Oh, you cannot speak so that people will get what you desire to say.

You must speak from your heart, for that is the only vehicle that reveals the truth.

People do not want a finely tuned, slickly oiled machine that spurts out words of wisdom from a perfectly packaged past. They want a woman who is truly honest.

If you go to therapy, ten or twenty years later you finally say, "Ohh, I discovered how screwed up I am and now I know why! Because my parents were not there for me." Fifty-thousand dollars in therapy sessions and what you come up with is the reason why you have not allowed yourself to shine, followed through on projects, been bold and audacious (your words) in your life (and I do not mean you, Lysa, I mean the people of this world) and all you can come up with is that mommy wasn't there for you or daddy never paid attention and that's why you're so screwed up!

Your parents were wherever they were and you didn't like where that happened to be. You thought since you were their kid, you should have a say (and boy did you say) on where they should choose to be.

Did you ever notice that wherever your parents were, it was never okay for them to be?

What are you saying, that the world is infused with a pack of spoiled brats?

No, but close. What I am saying is the people whom you seek to assist, the ones who have lost a loved one to suicide or have thought/attempted to kill themselves, these are the people packed with ideas about how the past (and present for that matter) should and should not be.

Life is what it is. The past is over. It's done. If you did not like the way it turned out, then why would you continue to speak of it?

Let today be the start of your life. Let each moment be the start of your destiny.

November 15, 1999

JOSEPH: If a person is depressed, the only reason they would choose suicide is because they have some notion, conscious or not, that they should not be depressed. They think that being depressed is not a state in which they should choose to be.

How did they learn that? Where did that notion come from? Their parents?

Could be. I'm not interested in tracing the roots back to their parents. In this day and age, that is an extreme cop out for taking responsibility for your life. Parents did this. Parents did not do this. I was not held enough. I was held too much. When the mind wants to be right, it will always come up with ways to make another wrong.

What do you mean?

I mean that given the state in which we live, the world in which we live, we are bombarded daily with messages of what NOT to do.

Don't do drugs, don't drink and drive, don't be mean, don't steal, don't lie, don't cheat. We are told thousands of times a day what it is the world expects us not to do. Then we are bombarded with messages of all the bad things people have done. They've killed, cheated, lied, stole, did drugs, drank, abused their spouse, and so on.

So first we are told what NOT to do, then we are told of all the people who did what they were instructed NOT to do.

This is what is being programmed into the minds of our youth. This is what they see each night as their family watches the evening news. This is the great, or not so great, tragedy of the human race. We believe what is written in newspapers, what we see on the news, and when it comes from someone with the post initials Ph.D or M.D., we believe it even more.

What can I do about this?

Educate the public on that which you know to be true. Not true in the absolute "this is the way it is" sense of the word, but true in an alternative way of looking at things.

You see, there is no "true." Even the notion that we all will die, this is only true in the abstract of what we now know to be true about death.

There is no death once you experience what it is to die. Yet saying this to those who have not yet crossed over may seem arrogant or preposterous. We are not likely to take in that which seems foreign to us. This is why the concept of vegetarianism is foreign to some people, especially to children. In school, children are taught only what the world decides is right for them to be taught. They are offered a distorted and piece-meal view of the world, one that does not threaten their belief system.

How did it get to be this way?

The world became more and more complex, not in its nature, but in its perception. We began to see that one television was not enough, so we purchased three. Then we needed cable, then a T.V. blocker so the youngsters could not watch the violent shows. Then we got a DVD, a VCR, a satellite dish, a computer with T.V. access, and so on.

Our needs, or rather, our perception of our needs, became expanded with each new purchase until what we had in our houses became too much to maintain and we either sold it all or stored it away. Also, we blame so much.

We blame the world for the complexity of what it offers. Twenty kinds of diet soda, distilled water, mineral water, spring water, oxygen-enhanced water, sparkling water, fruity water... This is what we're up against when we go to the grocery store.

But instead of looking at it as a blessing of abundant selection, we make choosing into a problem and blame it on all the things, too many things, which are available for us to choose.

We actually think the variety of water is the problem. We, up here, see you as having an awesome selection of purchases to make.

You call it a problem.

We call it a party.

It's all in your perception, in how you perceive your world.

You cannot defeat your purpose here on earth. You can only fail to realize what it is.

And if you DO realize what it is, you can only fail to take steps toward achieving and fulfilling it.

And if you DO take steps toward achieving and fulfilling it, you can only fail to take steps that offer you your outcome.

And if you do take steps that offer you your outcome, you may not realize that by the time you get what you think you wanted, what you wanted has already changed.

We change just like that?

Yep. This is how it works… You do, do, do…

You get focused, centered, and passionate about what you're about to embark on, about the path you've finally chosen to take.

And then you take it. You get on the road and you drive.

And you drive and drive and drive, and you're singing in your car, and you're smiling out your window, and you're close to your desired destination, almost there, after driving for days in the hot sun with no sleep, you're almost about to get to the very place on which you have set your sights, but then...

BAM!!!

A boulder hits your car.

Now, you're screwed.

No money.

No place to stay.

You don't know what to do.

Do you throw in the towel and forget the whole thing or do you find a way to get your car on track and continue on your journey?

Are you asking me?

JOSEPH: No, I'm telling you this... Right before you are about to receive everything you've ever desired, dreamed about, and envisioned in your mind, there will be a catastrophe – a test.

Make sure the readers are paying attention because these are the laws of life. When you're just about to hit the big time, a boulder will fall on your car in order to see what you will do.

Do you give up? Sell out? Lose a bit of your enthusiasm? Or do you forge ahead with an even greater strength, knowing that there is nothing outside that you cannot handle, nothing too big to break your peace of mind.

Sylvester Stallone was tested. With a pregnant wife and less than $100 in the bank, he was offered $300,000 NOT to star in his film 'Rocky.'

"No way," he said. He saw himself as the star and did not sell out.

He waited, not passively mind you, not with the underlying belief that he was making the biggest mistake of his life.

He waited with the knowing that the goods he had seen so clearly in his mind, were on their way.

He had the truest kind of belief, the kind where nothing exists behind the belief. It's the purest kind when you say what is so, even if the outside world has not yet manifested it.

Everything is possible. You say that on your business cards, Lysa.

I'm not sure if I always believe it.

Most of the time you do.

The bottom line is that we must take the time to find out what we require in order to feel fulfilled. Then we must find out what others need, from themselves and from us in order to feel fulfilled, and then we must support them on their mission.

Most of us are so me, me, me, me, me. What will happen if I do this? What will not happen if I do not? Most of our conversations are geared toward ourselves. If not directly, then indirectly, or rather, manipulatively through covert conversations around what it is we really desire to say. We don't say it like it is, we say it like we think people desire to hear it.

We second-guess people all the time, saying what we think they want to hear, instead of what we truly desire to express.

We act one way with our parents, another with our friends, another with our kids, another with our spouse, another with our coworkers, and another with our dog. No wonder we have so many schizophrenics in this world. We are all split off in a multitude of directions and we have lost track of how to find our way home.

Why do we fear people so much?

VERTITUDE: Because we are afraid of being found out. You heard the guy last week at your seminar say he finally came out to his family that he was gay and when he did, they all said, "We already knew."

Everybody knows, but most are too afraid to reveal what they know. Most of the stuff we fear happening to us, never does.

November 18, 1999

I feel like I have spent the whole day doing bullshit when I really want to spend my time writing to you. Writing with you.

VERTITUDE: No you don't.

Why do you say that?

If you did, then you would. If you did not, then you would not. It is as simple as that. But it is too simple for you complex human beings who always need to find an excuse as to why they did not do what they said they really desired to do.

It is impossible to truly BE when you are not BEING who you truly are.

What you must know is that the ego does not exist. It was made up by the language not emplaced in the human soul.

When you were born, there was no "ego." How could there have been without the use of language? How could you be without the use of language? You only know yourself to be you because what it is you say is you is done through the use of language. There is no you without the word you. There is no not you without the words, "There is no not you."

So my point is for you to understand that all whom shall transpire through the gates of Heaven, not heaven as in up here high in the sky, but heaven as in the heaving of your soul. To be with whatever is, you must first be clear on what is and what is not.

What is, is.
What is not, is not.
You is.
Got it?

Yes.

Good. Now what is living and what is death? What is love and what is hate? What is a boy and what is a girl? What is a success and what is a failure? What is a good day and what is a bad one?

If you cannot be with who you are being in every moment, you cannot be with who you are not being in every moment. There is no use in being against whom you are being when you are being it.

It is like eating a potato chip and while you are eating it, you are being angry with yourself for eating it. What is the use of that? The use is our insane thinking that if I am beating myself up for what I am doing then I will never do it again. Of course, you do it again. You always do it again.

Why? Not for the reason you think.

Why? Because hatred never begets love.

Why? Because transformation comes from loving oneself so deeply, so passionately, that nothing else can coexist.

Darkness and light cannot coexist.

You can have dimness.

But neither darkness nor light can be categorized as dimness.

Dimness is dimness.

Darkness is darkness.

Light is light.

There can be a dark corner, a dim corner and a light corner. But inside of each corner is only what is, and not what is not. Inside of the lighted corner is light. In the light, in the very essence, the very place that light exists, exists light, not darkness, not dimness. Do you understand the importance of this?

Yes.

VERTITUDE: Who are you when you are at your highest? Who are you when you are at your best? Do you ever know what your best is? Will you ever have the capacity to know what your best is whilst you are still living in a body on this earth?

The energy just shifted. Satori just walked in and the energy shifted. Why is that? What is the cause of the energy shifting?

VERTITUDE: The energy shifting is the cause of the energy shifting. Energy shifts. You shift. He shifts. The energy in the room is dependent upon who is ruling the universe at any moment.

What I mean by that is simple. Energies rule the universe. Who you are rules the universe. Who you are being is strong or weak according to what game you are playing in the world. If you are playing small or meek, you will be overburdened by the intensity of energy in someone who is playing strong and solid.

You overpower those who are small and meek?

At times we do this. It wakes them up and brings them to see that which has not been seen in themselves… in their lives.

We seek to have people respect us when we do not even respect ourselves. We seek for people to pay us monies that we would never pay ourselves. We seek for approval where we have none inside. In the world in which you now live there is little knowing about who people are and what they desire, need, and require to proficiently prosper and flourish in this world.

You people are so caught up in what you want or desire that you never take the time to find out what the other person wants, truly wants, beneath their asking, beneath their words of desire.

You must learn to read the silence of the human soul. This is where all the magic of the universe exists. This is what the world you have created for yourself requires in order for you to be extraordinary, as if who you really are could be anything else.

What you do when you act unlike your true self is that you put on a costume and then expect people to see through the fabric of your scheme. You relate to people as if they are the costumes they wear.

This is as ludicrous as greeting someone who is wearing a Hawaiian shirt and thinking who they are is a Hawaiian shirt and not a person wearing a Hawaiian shirt.

Why are people so hard on themselves?

They are not.

What they are is conditioned to act in ways that provoke harshness. They feel bad for not feeling bad. It's like a funeral. You are supposed to feel bad, right? Something is wrong with you if you do not feel bad, especially if the person who has died was your son or daughter or spouse or parent. This is the call for feeling bad in your culture and just like a well-trained puppy, what you do is act accordingly.

What would happen if your grief at losing someone you love sprung from the well of its own creation and not from the preconceived ideas of society which tell you how to feel, when to feel it, and how long to feel it for.

What would happen if how you felt were truly a direct reflection of how YOU felt? If you love someone and they die, or worse, take their own life, then how are you supposed to feel?

If you suffer, day after day, replaying the gruesome details of their death, who suffers?

You do.

Why?

Because you think that it's going to eventually bring you some relief. It's like, if you suffer enough, you will someday be cleansed of all your self-created sins. To sin literally means to miss the mark. We all miss the mark sometimes.

Suffering does not change what we did. It only brings more pain to the future of our existence.

What happens to souls when we mourn their death in a manner that causes us suffering?

They suffer.

If we suffer, they suffer.

I say we because I am a higher spirit, one who has gone before the spirits who have recently crossed over. They are like children to me.

So when they are in pain, I am in pain. If you are in pain on earth, then your loved one who took his or her own life is in pain to the direct proportion you are. Actually, that's not true. They suffer more.

Why?

Because they have committed the act against themselves. They would be freed more quickly if you healed your pain, rather than relived it year after year.

What does it do to your heart when you mourn for years? How can you be in the presence of love when you are absorbed in the throes of pain? Self-inflicted pain is what your loved one put upon themselves when they chose to die.

Why do you not think your pain and suffering is any different than theirs? They ended their life. You are refusing to live yours by remaining in regret and pain. So what can you do?

You can understand what has transpired by understanding that your life can be the continuation of theirs. Your progress can lead them forth... along their way.

Look inside your soul and ask yourself, "For whom are you suffering? Is it for the person who has gone or is it for whom has been left behind?

My hands are hurting from writing.

Your hands are hurting right now because the pressure on them is due to the presence of a force unnatural to you.

You are not used to probing so deeply beneath the layers of psychological bullshit into an arena that is all your own.

Your soul is a stadium of epic proportions able to hold all, everything.

What you must do in times like these is remember that there are no other times than these.

Do you get what I am saying here?

Lysa, you are a chosen vehicle, not for this moment, but for all eternity. You have been chosen over and over again for your keen insight and ability to take what is handed to you and make it beautiful.

What is it I am writing here? Why do I always want to stop before I am done?

Why? Because what you are doing will never be done. You stop to save yourself from the pain of working forever.

You see, you already know the infinite capacity of the human mind to experience the eternity of the world in THIS MOMENT! In this instant!

Right now you could experience and have all you have ever wanted! Right now you can be that which you seek to be at some later date.

To the human race, NOW is never a good time to get things done.

I mean really get things done.

Profound things like cleaning up this nation, sweeping up the world. A mental sweep would do us well. Get one of those computer programs, like Norton Clean Sweep. How about that on the minds of human beings? Clean sweep their brains. Do away with all that shit they've been fed and create a clean slate from which they can begin anew.

Right now you must call your father. You said you would call him tonight and tonight is now tonight. This is what I mean. Now is never a good time in which can be done.

You can use that when you counsel people who are suicidal. Ask them if they ever procrastinate? Of course, 99% of them will say yes.
Then ask them to procrastinate death, to put it off. Put it off until it no longer seems like a feasible thing to do. Like getting a tattoo after seeing a Grateful Dead concert, if you hold out for a week or so, the urge usually goes away.

Not to make a suicidal person's tendencies less than what they are—a tragic cry for help—but in the scheme of things, of life, one must understand one's control over one's destiny, no matter what the doctors tell them.

What is the power and importance of listening?

You cannot hear that which you do not listen to. You must experience the speaking of your soul, of another's soul.

You must fully express all that is within and offer others the chance to express the things they fear to say.

In the presence of those willing to listen, you will be healed. In the presence of offering others the chance to fully speak, they will be healed.

You cannot wish for another to bare their soul and then punish or judge them for what they have revealed. You must make a pact that whatever is said remains sacred and true. You must offer sanctity to the person whose heart you are asking to share and offer comfort in their time of desperation, isolation, fear, and trepidation.

But you must first give yourself permission to speak fully. There is nothing worse than an adult who dares not to begin. We must all be willing to be a beginner, to take that first step, yet most fear doing so.

We are a society of experts, expecting to have been that way since the time of our birth.

Where is the room for learning?

Where has all the beginner's gone? If one cannot begin, where does that leave those who have not yet begun?

You must offer yourself permission to begin. Anything that lights your heart on fire - Begin it now.

Anything that causes the angels in your heart to sing - Begin it now.

No other person can begin for you that which is your job to begin. No other soul can master for you that which is your job to master.

In the attainment of mastery, there is a time of beginning. Like the colt that awkwardly learns to walk, you must grant yourself permission and complete freedom to begin and begin over and over again and again.

What causes differences amongst people?

The unwillingness to HEAR people, really hear what people have to say. Most of the time we are not listening to people when they speak. We are instead, preparing in our minds exactly what we are going to say.

139

No wonder people do not feel heard.

Oh, you do not need a person to listen to you in order to feel heard. You can transcend the need of the listener to listen and speak as though every word you utter has a time and a place in which it is heard.

What do you mean by this?

No matter what the world looks like, it is not as it seems. The world contains many dimensions, some small, some vast. The world in which you live is relatively small compared to the world where I reside.

When you see the world through a telescope, you can only see what is within the scopes range. Nothing outside of its realm exists for you. It's the same with others.

If their scope does not match yours, conflict arises. You cannot understand why they don't see what you see. You cannot understand why they see themselves in the way they do.

You see their greatness.

They see their pain.

You see their magnificence.

They see their flaws.

What can I do to widen my scope of the world?

Open your eyes.

SEE.

LOOK.

DISCOVER.

EVERYTHING…. YOU HAVE EVER WANTED TO SEE IS THERE. CLOSE YOUR EYES AND SEE IT NOW.

You want to take that Hawaiian vacation, close your eyes and go there now.

You desire to win an Academy Award, close your eyes and win it now.

What else is there except the memories you hold in your mind? And the experiences you hold in your heart, those you have had and those you will have. They're all there now. Just not in the way you think they are.

What is heaven's consensus on depression?

JAY (age 35): We choose it.

No, not like we go to the local diner and say, "I'd like some eggs, bacon, and an order of depression, the clinical kind, extra strength, the one that kills you."

In choosing it, I now know that I used my mind, what I focused on, what I believed, to further perpetuate my depressed state.

This disease, as they now call it, is something that gets people completely off the hook as having any responsibility for their state of mind. Calling it a disease also lets them, the doctors, parents, and society, off the hook because if one has a disease, then one is sick and surely it is the bodies fault, the biochemistries fault, and not theirs.

Now, look at this. Look at this carefully. HOW CONVENIENT IS IT TO PLACE RESPONSIBILITY UPON SOMETHING THAT CANNOT TALK.

The body, yes it speaks in aches, pains, joy, and sorrow, yet it cannot talk back to a doctor. It cannot assume responsibility without the owner assuming it (through the use of language) for him or herself. The body is neutral. It just "gets sick." Well, wouldn't ya know! What a damn pain in the ass, but no worries, it's not my fault, it's my body's fault.

Sure, if I chow down cow meat and carbohydrates filled with refined sugar, hold in my emotions and hate my job and my wife and my life, it will surely not result in my body hating to be the vessel for me.

What, do you think the body is stupid, so stupid that it will not break down if I what I put in it is shit?

A car would last longer running on ice cream than our bodies should last with all the shit we put in them, and that includes our thoughts, whether verbalized or not.

We are a society bent on believing what the other guy says. If the other guy is rich, high powered, and has certain initials or sets of initials next to his or her name, preferably M.D., then we believe them.

We are so bent on believing people with degrees, that we often don't take a look at how these people live their lives. We don't check out if they actually practice what they profess.

When doctors speak of depression, or any disease for that matter, as something we <u>get</u> rather than something we <u>create</u>, it puts enormous pressure on our insides to maintain our role of victim and not of conqueror.

You see, if we play no role in having our lives not work, our bodies not work.

What kind of role can we then play in having our lives work? Is that it?

Yes. Either we have power or we do not.
I'm so glad you don't live in victimhood.

That section of town is rather crowded right
now, don't you think?

So you see, it's because those who sell the drug
of denial in one's power and ability to heal thyself, who
have spoken much louder than those who have
successfully conquered diseases without the traditional
use of drugs.

We must educate people. Educate them to look
further, deeper, more carefully, about what is being
shown to them.

I mean, we were taught, "Doctor knows best."
So we have learned to follow the orders given by the
doctor, written on the prescription, without question.

Isn't it strange that despite being in a locked
psychiatric ward, receiving the 'best' medical attention
money can buy, I attempted to kill myself.

I was in on a 48-hour suicide watch and
managed to bribe the nurse to give me an extra blanket
when I said I was cold.

The main blanket was actually attached to the
bed with an alarm set to it so that if I attempted to pull
it off the bed, the alarm would sound and the nurses
would come running. But this nurse bought into my

plea for warmth and gave me an extra blanky, which I promptly used to hang myself.

If that same nurse hadn't been so God damn nice, coming back to check on me, to see if I was warm enough, I would have died.

She walked in just as I kicked the chair out from under my feet. That God damn caring nurse screwed up my entire suicide. Of course, I got her back. I got them all back. I did it again, later.

This time in the privacy of my own home, using a showerhead rather than a beam and a lock on my door, my phone off the hook, and my mind on hold, as I gathered the courage to take away my life.

What do you know now that you didn't know then?

That I have all the power within myself to lead the life I truly desire, to create that which I have now envisioned in my mind and to continue creating the images and language through which I express my highest goals. I had it all along, this knowing. I just didn't pay attention to it. I don't know how much louder my soul could have screamed.

For God sakes, I was an alcoholic and cocaine addict. How much louder can your soul speak its pain?

I tested the outer limits of normalcy just to score drugs in the middle of the night.

What was I thinking? I wasn't. My soul was crying, "Help me! Listen to me! I need your help! Is anybody home? Is anyone there to help me?"

Of course, no one was home.

Here, write this letter for me.

Dear Mr. Ovitz,

I know you are saddened by the death of your former close friend and brother for life, Jay Moloney. And I know the sorrow which has set upon your heart in not knowing, or rather, not being aware of the extent that he needed to be known in order for you to do something to save his life.

Actually, there is no saving of lives that goes on in heaven or in earth—there are just people who stick around, look closely, keep a keen eye on those with whom they have bonded. They never allow pettiness or bitter angry discrepancies to get in the way of their love. The other night you were in the presence of the men with whom you began your journey. From creating CAA to your stint at Disney, your endeavor into a theater house, and now, your succession of brilliance is planted upon an organization called AMG.

Jay was someone with whom you could tell anything. In the best of times, he was closer to you than you were to yourself. In the worst, he was like a nagging pet or annoying bug, a butterfly perhaps, one that had not yet formed into what it was capable of becoming. He was a caterpillar still left with its soggy middle, not yet knowing exactly how to fly.

You flew.

You knew how to fly so well, so you taught those who didn't know the dynamics and mechanics of flying, how to follow your lead.

You did it brilliantly, respectfully, and did it until you didn't desire to do it any longer. This is what Jay did. He did life until he didn't want to do life anymore.

This letter comes from a place that I cannot yet fully describe. All I can say is that I am certain of your love for Jay and that he wants you to know how special you were to him.

He remembers the glamorous life that you led, the people with whom you spoke, the parties you frequented, and most of all, the private moments you shared in the confines of your office, when all was quiet and brilliant and unique and the sun went down in the West toward the beach and you looked outside your window, maybe put a gentle arm around him, reassuring him of who he was to you.

To him, you were a father, mentor, coach, player, and friend. He was important to you in more ways then you allowed yourself to express to him. He knows that you have always cared, that you will always care.

You have remembered your place on this earth. Unfortunately, he did not. But now, I challenge you to this: Communicate where you have not communicated.

Step up where you have allowed yourself to step down. Come from authenticity, boldness, and love. I was guided to write you this letter. No response or reply is necessary.

Make peace with the partners you left behind. For your power and your strength is contained within the duty of your action, the honor of your word, and the virtue of your heart. The strongest man is one who can also be meek. The more courageous man is one who needs not roar. And the most powerful soul is one who can transcend anything and take from life, nothing, yet give back to life, all that life has not given him.

To teach is to demonstrate, which is why you were the best teacher for Jay.

He loved life when he was around you. Always know that, remember that, and relish it within your heart. — Love, L.M. written by J.M.

"One cannot awaken in another
that which is not
awake within themselves."

November 21, 1999

I sit here, ready to write and step out of my room for a moment. I meet my mother in the hallway and she says, "You told me you and Satori would find your own place by the end of the holidays."

"I know," I tell her.

She asks if I am mad.

I hold back my tears and say no.

Then I turn and walk away. She mentions something about taking my mail up to her room by mistake. I look toward her, but not at her, and say, "It's okay."

I go into my room, her office, and sit here and write. The feeling in my throat is one of tightness. I feel like I could have been there more for her in living here.

149

Asked her how she was feeling. Spending more time in her room.

But for what? The sole purpose of connecting with my mother?

No.

This is not what makes me write this, for in connecting with my mother, I do not have a problem. I love her so much and love to connect with her daily, on the phone, when we went to the Suicide Prevention conference yesterday.

What I am talking about is guilt connection. The kind of connection that occurs when I think I should be doing something I am not. The kind of connection that comes from a place of complacency and fear, rather than contribution and strength.

The feelings I have inside come from my unwillingness to DO something with my life that the world thinks I should do.

Get a job.

Go to work.

Go to the gym.

Eat right.

Don't say that.

Don't do this.

Who am I writing to right now?

Who am I talking with?

Me.

Who?

Jay.

Jay who?

You know.

I know that I know. Just say it.

Jay M_____. They are having my funeral today. I couldn't stay there any longer. It's too depressing.

What is?

Them. They have no idea who I really was and now they profess to have all this insight about me; insight even I didn't have.

What are you going to do?

Write through you.

Why me?

Because you'll do it, plus, I need the help.

I will allow you to speak through me on one condition.

What is that?

You do not drain and zap my energy of my psychic presence with your need to finish or fulfill whatever it is you left undone on this earth. Also, stay away from Satori, Siobhan, and my mom, and leave your friends up there, up there.
Do not bring anyone else into the presence of our conversation and when we are through you leave, leaving nothing, no residue or unfinished business or anger at being cut off, here. Do you understand and agree to these conditions?

Yes. I promise.

Good. Now tell me everything.

I was feeling lost and alone in my life, even though hundreds, literally hundreds of people surrounded me daily. I still felt alone.

I did not know how to express it to my coworkers, who were seemingly stoked at having everything their eager hearts could desire—money, so much money, prestige, the ability to hobnob with the rich and famous.

Boy Lysa, you are really avoiding this conversation. You just formatted close to fifty pages.

Thirty-five. And yes, I am avoiding it and thanks for letting the readers know.

Now I'm going to get really insulted. You put on a sweatshirt, half-close the window; dust off your "Leap of Faith" sign.

You are going to get really insulted? It means you are not insulted yet, but you are planning to get that way or feel insulted in the near future. Why not plan a vacation instead of planning to get insulted?

I should have known you when I was alive. I think, I know, you could have saved my life.

Don't say that.

Why not?

Because it is always easier to say what you think would have happened when there is no way to validate or verify if what you said is true because what is in the past cannot be changed.

This is true. Maybe you should pass the word on about this. Many people are living like what they did in the past can be undone.

Nothing exists except for right now and right now and right now. Do you get what I am saying?

I wish I had cut through the bullshit of my life, when I was conversing with some "big wig" in Hollywood and when they asked me a question and I didn't give a shit about what they had asked because whatever it was, the answer was going to be yes.

Yes because I was interested in working with them. Yes, because I was interested in being their friend. Yes, because I was lonely.

Yes, because I wanted to score drugs. Yes, because I wanted to be a big shot.

Yes, because I wanted to look good. Yes, because I wanted them to like me. Yes, because, because, because, because... We're off to see the wizard, the wonderful wizard of Oz.

You're funny. Thank you. Honest too.

That's a first. No one, and I mean this when I say no one has ever referred to me as being honest. A sleaze bag, conniver, con artist, quick talker, mighty mouse, and big dumbo, which my brother Darren called me.

I am in limbo now because I have cut my journey on this earth short. Remember the saying, be careful for what you ask for because you may get it? I did. I was so damn lucky to have Michael Ovitz as my mentor and leader of my career in Hollywood.

But I blew it.

Literally.

I had a million dollars in the bank by age thirty and had men and women falling at my feet. Men excited me more, but up here there is no such thing as straight or gay. So I am off the hook with all that crap. But down there, I had an identity crisis to go along with my drug habit.

I would speak to people in Hollywood and say that which I knew they wanted to hear. I mastered the art of the perfect word—the bullshit of knowing what to say, whom to say it to, and how to respond when they spoke to me.

I had to move around a lot of shit without them knowing. Act like they got the money they asked for, no problem, by a director who thought they were a piece of shit. I had to make it look like everyone in Hollywood loved each other, when in reality, when all heads were turned and even when some were not, they, most of them, majority of them, hated each others guts.

Now, being where I am, from this "newfound" perspective, I see that all their hatred is just a cover-up for fear. They are merely afraid of exposing their souls because of what they think might occur as a result of their honesty about who they are, about what really matters to them, about how truly fearful they feel about losing everything they have worked so hard to attain.

Hollywood, and the rest of the world for that matter, is one big façade. A cover-up for what is truly necessary to cast away the pain.

We think that by hiding ourselves we are protecting the world from what we perceive to be the gruesomeness of our soul.

In reality what we are doing is leaving everyone to feel alone. It is a hideously cruel game we play with one another on earth.

How do you get others past their façade of fear?

By getting past your façade.

What is the difference between a rat and a human?

A rat will go into a maze looking for the cheese hidden at the end of the last tunnel. If the cheese is moved, the rat will go down the original tunnel several times and then try another tunnel until the rat finds the cheese.

A human will find the cheese down the first tunnel then continue to go down the same tunnel, even when the cheese has been moved.

You see rats are interested in finding cheese. Humans, adults mainly, are not so much interested in finding cheese, as they are interested in being right. "It was down there a minute ago. I know I am right. I saw the cheese. They couldn't have moved it. It couldn't have been moved. Let me just check three-thousand more times to make sure."

This is the insidious nature of the human being. They believe something is a certain way, even if it no longer is.

Don't you see the mind power and amount of mental time it takes in hiding and avoiding that which needs, is required to be done, in order for you to live happily in the world.

All of the mental energy it takes to suppress a feeling, a thought, a belief in ones ability to shine, is not close to a quarter of the energy of what it would take to allow you to soar.

When people like me kill themselves, we get a glimpse into the idiotic maneuvers we humans are capable of engaging in.

The moment I got done hanging myself, there was no more physical pain. Mental pain, yes, that was there, but a different sort.

I just made the biggest mistake of my life.

That's what caused me pain.

Seeing my body hanging there.

That's what caused me pain.

Watching Ben, my friend's face as it came through the bathroom door.

That's what caused me pain.

For the first time in my life, I truly knew what it felt like to be in another's shoes. Only now that I had this strange awakening, there was nothing I could do to turn back the clock, to use what I had learned in my life once more.

There was no more once more. I had used up my privilege to walk upon this earth. Regret cannot even describe the immensity of what I felt.

In that moment, I learned that pain only occurs in the looking back on events, in the reliving of them, over and over again. Recreating them in the now.

I was a player in Hollywood, not because I was so much better than others who sought to take my place, but because I was destined to achieve greatness, a level of greatness, which I now know, doesn't account for much in Heaven.

Love, that's what scores points. Self-love, first, and from that flows love for all living things.

What was it like at your memorial service?

Wild. A bunch of big guys bawling their eyes out for a guy they hardly knew, barely tolerated, and definitely thought of with disgust.

How do you know this to be true?

One of the benefits of being in heaven, or between heavens (on earth and up here) is the ability to read a person's mind. I have that ability way more than I had it while on earth.

You had it while on earth?

Yes, we all do. You do to a larger extent than many. But we all have the ability to be with multiple people, in multiple places, and with a variety of energy waves, at all times. We know so much yet most of us are not willing to acknowledge just how much we know to be true.

This is true.

Thank you for acknowledging that.

Back to your memorial service. What was it like?

Spooky, weird. It was weird to see all of my "friends" packed into a theater like it was a Hollywood premiere and hear their voice crack and eyes shed tears as they spoke of me.

Underneath my Armani suits and Ray Ban glares, I was one frightened cookie. They saw through it, some of them. That's what I'm talking about, the knowing that you know that you know. People know so much about what's going on, they just don't trust what they know.

What they know may not be easily translated into words, but it's a knowing all its own. If they went with the feeling, whatever it was, they would find themselves at a place of knowing where everything they had once thought was real was now not, and everything they feared to be true, was actually a lie.

There is a place within us, each of us, where all that is true, remains true.

You are losing your connection with me because you seek to listen to what Satori is saying on the phone. You fear the call is for you and fear that in a moment you will be interrupted and have to stop writing.

Is it not amazing how much time is wasted in worrying about what we think will happen?

You are writing now at a level of pure unconsciousness, so just allow your fingers to hit the keys and you will be surprised at what you see, for in the realm of the unconscious lies all the secrets to what you came here for. These will not be discovered in a book, not even in this book.

Yes, certain truths will be revealed here, but this is not where people will find their truth. In the language called words, one cannot connect to the souls version of language that is complete without words.

This is the "gut" instinct of which I speak. This is the silent killer that if not heeded and acted upon, will sever the ties that bond you and another person, you and the entirety of the world. What it is that you must do is this - You must become that which you seek to be.

You cannot be becoming something and simultaneously be that. You are already it. It is already you. In this stance of knowingness, you set forth and act from a place of who you are at your highest and best.

There is no future time or date that is better for you to become who you really are. That's the big joke in life; that we people seek, oh so diligently seek, to become the very thing we already are.

It is as you said to that girl in the car last night as she was speaking to you regarding searching for the man, the ideal man of her dreams. She had made her ideal mate list, had checked to see if these qualities she sought in another were already vital within herself, and then set forth on a journey, a mission actually, a manhunt more appropriately, to find this mate she said would complete her world.

Now you said this to her. "Be the woman who already has found and is in relationship with that ideal mate. How would you be if he were already in your life? You must be it in every sense of the word.

This is the key.

We think that the thing, the money, success, person, brings with it the okay for us to be all that we desire to be. We live in a perpetual state of "Just wait until…" or "When that happens or arrives, then I will be, feel, allow myself to stop doing…".

Hello! Is anybody out there? Did anyone hear of Elvis or Marilyn or River or me? I am the perfect example of the man who had everything/nothing and thought his existence on earth was no longer worthwhile. I was shit in my book, the book I had written called "my pitiful, sorry ass, poor me life."

And guess what? This was the only book I read. I spent my days and nights reading my shitty book of what I perceived to be my meaningless life.

But boy did my life look good. Just like a shiny apple, which on the outside looks prime and juicy, but then you cut it open and find worms.

I was filled with the crud of the earth, the inescapable, pitiful pain of martyrdom. "Poor me! Poor me!" the apple cries out. "Why don't you see the rotting of my soul? Why did you not cut open my skin and take away the worms?"

"Because I could not see the pain I was in," answers the apple. I could not see past myself."

People judge others with the parameters from which they judge themselves. There is no separation between how I say you think of me and how I say I think of me. Whatever I hold to be true in my mind becomes, literally becomes my truth out in the world.

It's as if there is nothing between us—nothing, nothing, that separates my mind from yours, not really.

There is nothing that escapes my thoughts that cannot ooze into the thoughts you hold about me. What is important is for us to understand the power of our thoughts and the impact they have on what happens in our world.

How is it that we are blind to so much good in the world? How is it that we cannot see what is out there to serve us, has been serving us? Why are we so blind to the miracles offered to us in our lives?

WE ARE NOT BLIND.

There are only things we choose not to see.

It is a choice, this not seeing thing. It is a conscious choice to look away from what is in front of us. We actually spend our time looking for what's not there—what's missing. In the powerful sense of this, it is important to determine or distinguish what's not there so we can find the means in which to replace it or fill it with something which serves us, serves others, and serves the greater good.

But in the world of what we know as looking for what's missing, we are clueless on how to use this power of distinction. We look for what's missing just for the hell of it!

Let me see what I can find wrong in my life today, is the methodology behind how we often operate in the world. Let me see what I can find wrong in another person. Let me see how many things I can come up with to validate the self-perception that they are providing for me.

You see, everything we see or do not see in another is a direct reflection of what we are not willing to look at within ourselves.

THERE IS NO ONE OUT THERE. That's the big mask of it all - thinking something is out there. It's like the man in the crazy house—the house of mirrors I think they call it, who runs through this maze of mirrors, scared at times by the reflection he sees, forgetting, if only for a split second, that the reflections he sees are his own.

There is nothing outside of us from which we can take—only give. There is no one in the universe that can be more for us than we are willing to be for ourselves. That is the great gift of mentors or having a teacher who inspires us to be at the level of being which we are ready to step up to be. They show for us that which we will be showing to the world from ourselves, from within ourselves.

I don't understand what you just said.

Yes you do. You say you don't understand, when in actuality, you do.

Look! Look closer.

Remember the things you learned at the courses you just completed. When you think you know or think you do not know, before you really take a look at what it is you're attempting to know—in those times, you are a fool being foolish in your quickness of thought and action.

People are so quick to say that they know something is true when if they would just take the time and look at it—from every angle if necessary, they would discover that what they thought to be true is not.

Then we would have a world of equality, not in the way you have grown accustomed to looking at the word, but in the way of common or equal respect, admiration, and reverence for every living thing on this earth.

What you choose to do with the knowledge you have is up to you.

What you choose to do with what has been bestowed upon you in the most gracious way is up to you.

Nothing, but a profound gratitude for having someone open the doors to your heart and soul is required in accumulating the wealth you say is necessary to create that which you seek to create in the world.

Nothing kills a persons desire to assist you more than a lack of gratitude, not the kind that says, "Thanks a lot" or even a formal "thank you."

The kind that oozes up from your belly button onto the ends of your heart, then washes away all that is cruddy in the realm of hardness in your heart and replaces it with a sense of soft grace and tenderness, none of which can be replaced or taken away from someone other than you.

You are the maker of your world, keeper of the safe, and designer of your realm.

We walk around acting like the world is doing it to us. And then we get righteous and pissed off because people are not helping us the way they promised to and maybe we whine, can you hear a bit of a whine down there?

"It's not fair!" goes the whine. "I'm such a good person. It's them! If only they would stick to what they said they would do, then everything would be okay."
BULLSHIT!

We live in a world of our own making then bitch because we, the designer, did not design it to be user-friendly. These days we are tired of blaming ourselves, so we blame others. Any others.

God, we blame God. That's a good one. Blame God, the ultimate in unreachable existence. God is not coming over to fix the sink as your plumber would, so why do you bitch to someone who cannot directly help you with your "problems?"

Why do you gossip to the girls at work about the man in your life that won't get a job? Talk to him! Of what service can others be in unraveling the web you have sewn for yourself? A listening board? Is that what your psychologist now tells you about the power of "getting things off your chest?"

There ain't nothing on your chest, except breasts if you're a woman, so there ain't nothing to get off your chest. Do you see how these metaphors literally ruin our lives?

Life is hard. Life's a bitch. Men suck. Men are great. I love all people because they love me. I hate that woman because she looked at me funny. Did you see the way she looked at me, honey? She kind of curled her lip and snarled at me. Did you see her do that? I'm never talking to her again. Screw her. Screw you. Screw the world. Screw me. Bang. It's all over. I won! You lost! I got out of the game before I could be kicked out. Phew. Wasn't that close?

I nearly drowned in the shit of my own making. I nearly fooled the world with my façade of glue. I was strong, stuck to everything, and was immovable.

No one could get to me when I was alive. I wasn't going to let those doctors, teachers, or friends see that what they said, affected me. No way. Not tough Jay. I was tough. If I showed them my pain, then they would win and I would lose, be the loser.

You see - I thought I had to die.

I thought I had to die because living would have meant they were right.

I was not going to play sick boy for anyone.

I was not a sicko. I was a boy who had lost his way. That's all that happened.

Somewhere between coloring books and building blocks, I forgot who I was and became whoever they wanted me to be. I became it so well that who I was, who I truly was, faded into the background like a leaf in the forest.

I felt dead.

I faded so far into the background that death was a feeling, a longing, a pulling; something was pulling me down, back.

I thought it was death calling my name.

I now know that I was wrong.

Death was not the one tugging on my veins. It was me, the old me, the original me. It was me all along, calling, shouting, "Come home Jay! Come back home!"

It was not death calling me. It was not death that called upon the people who have taken their lives. It was they who called upon death. Be patient with me, will you?

Please, all I ask is for your patience in knowing who I am at the deepest level. Will you take the time and get to know the 'real me' whom I have only recently met? Will you do that for me?

Yes. It is an honor to meet you Jay.

A bird is called a Jay Bird. What is the calling of this bird? From where they are called is where they will fly. They only fly in the direction of their calling, you know. They fly where the birds with which they flock, fly. They do not go against the mighty winds. They go with them or stop, allowing the winds to complete their course, before they take off again.

So much is un-communicated. So much is unexplained. Can you believe that we purchase something or rent something in this country and have the nerve to call it ours? We are on loan here. Everything in this universe is on temporary loan from whomever it is who created it.

So many things are left unexpressed. So much is left unsaid. Why?

You tell me why Lysa? Why do you not express that which is foremost on your mind? Why do you hold them in and then blame something, a headache, tiredness, stomachache, for your pain? What is it about expressing yourself completely to others that has you hold yourself back?

A story. A reason for why you do not do precisely what will free you, stretch you, unleash your soul.

What is between you and selling your screenplay? A story. It's always a story that stops us, and a crappy one at best.

A story of how afraid we are.

We have a story that acts like a crater in front of our car, and even though we have the woman or manpower to lift it, we don't. Why?

Because then we'd have no longer an excuse of why we do not go on our way. We'd have a clear path in which to speed ahead, until that is, the next crater is placed before us.

Then we will come to choice, our choice, always our choice, as to whether or not we will bitch about the crater, move the crater ourselves, ask someone to help us move the crater, or just give up, as I did. Is what I'm saying making sense?

Yes. To me it is, but to those who read this, will it?

Yes, because you are. If you explain things in ways that universally, people can get it. Guess what? People get it.

Just like when you explained to that woman in the car the other night, Julia, about the difference between waiting at a bus stop, hoping for the bus to come and waiting at the bus stop with the expectation that the bus will come. Then if it doesn't, you're surprised like, "What happened to the bus?" It was unexpected that it didn't come or if it comes late, you're surprised at that it came late. You don't expect it to, unless it continues to come late, then you begin to expect the bus to come late. The more times the bus is late, the more likely you are to expect it to be late the next time you're waiting.

Depending on your vision of the world and conditions of expectation, tolerance for it actually, will depend more or less on how quickly you become conditioned to expect the bus to come late. For some, it's after the bus is late once. For others, it takes a couple of times. And still for others, each time after the bus is late, they bitch at the bus, then expect it next time to be on time.

They bitch about having to wait for a bus that is late and when someone offers a suggestion, like why not take another bus, they come back with a stance that they will give this bus just one more time. Forever engaged in a perpetual state of blame and forgiveness, these people never see the impact they can have in causing the bus they take to actually begin to be on time. Maybe the bus is late for that very fact and no one out there is getting it.

Maybe it's late for someone to come along and train the bus driver, teach him or her, the importance of being on time. Maybe it's up to us to cause the solution of that which pisses us off.

Explain more about what I said about the woman waiting for the bus.

You explain it. You made it up.

Okay. I told this woman who was waiting for a man to show up in her life, that in her waiting, in her living

173

like something is missing and when it shows up then everything will okay, she was keeping in place that which was missing in her life.

That it's like waiting for the bus hoping it will arrive or waiting for it with an "Of course," attitude like, of course the bus will arrive.

You don't stand at the bus stop looking, hoping, and feeling agitated waiting for the bus to arrive. I'm not talking if you're late to be somewhere, and even then, we act like feeling agitated and nervous and looking at our watch will suddenly, supremely, make the bus appear, an ulcer maybe, but not the bus.

This has to do with the thought you just had while you were lighting the candle.

The thought was that, oh shit, I forgot the thought. There. Now I remembered. Thank you.

You're welcome.

The thought was that we are afraid to stand for something with such utter conviction because if it fails to happen, we fear we will feel crushed. So we are no longer dreamers who allow our hearts to be swept away by the verses in our souls. We are so fearful of being wrong.

Wrong or right are ways in which we devour our souls, the very essence of our being is a dichotomy. We are hot. We are cold. We are happy. We are sad. We are feeling sensual. We are feeling sour. We have so much to offer the world if just we would get out of our own way.

If we are to impact, influence, affect the world in which we live, we must live in the world as it is, live with people as they are, and not as we always think they ought to be.

What we must do to influence the world is to come from the premise that we make a difference. As that wonderful man Andrew Padilla said, "Each of you is a vegetable in a salad.

And you know how if you leave something out of a salad, if some vegetable is missing, the salad just doesn't taste the same. Well, that's how life is without you. Not the same."

I thought this was so powerful.

You didn't just think it was powerful, you told him it was powerful.

Yes, and at first I struggled with that, with whether or not to say something. As he was speaking of his daughter and his love for her and how when she was angry, she closed the door to her room and blasted music she thought he would hate and instead of hating it. Instead of allowing her to ruin his day, he danced.

The guy stood outside his angry daughter's bedroom and boogied to the beat. What an awesome man he was to do this and to give us a gift by sharing it with us.

"Being in your presence is a gift. It is an honor to be in your presence," I thought.

As tears welled up, I held myself back from expressing what I had just thought. "Why?" I asked myself silently. "What is it that frightens me about expressing gratitude to this man?" I held back for the rest of the speech, and then, just as he was about to close, I raised my hand.

He called on me.

I looked into his eyes, such tenderness in them and I expressed my gratitude with eloquence and love. He held me and showered his love right back into my soul. The love I had given was instantly returned, not only by him, but, by me.

You see how easy that was. Life is not about efforting. It's about being. Remember, we're beings. That's who we are.

Yes. This is what I was alluding to when I said earlier that all of us at some time or another have left behind our ability to feel passionately excited and certain about the destiny of which we can create.

Even writing those words, you choked on them.

Yes, why?

Because the moon is blue.

No. Tell me.

No. This is what I want you to say, that in this lifetime, you are meant to express yourself at the highest level. Nothing lower will do.

Tonight, I was reminded of the importance of noticing the signs… They are everywhere.
We must look with our eyes, not with those in front of our face, but those we cannot see, not in the typical sense of what it means to see.

177

Tonight I went to listen to a spiritual speaker talk about angels. He asked the group if we had ever had an experience with angels. I hesitated then raised my hand.

I spoke delicately of my experience writing this book. I hesitated, not in being embarrassed or worried about what to say, but more out of a respect for what has transpired here.

It has been said that the angels call upon EVERYBODY, yet not everybody cares to listen. Not because they really don't "care" but because they've been taught not to, that it's childish to believe in that which you cannot see.

I believe it is childish to only believe in that which you can see; for the mind escapes reality each time it enters a movie theater. As the lights go down, we are moved, touched, frightened, or inspired by the images and stories we see on the screen.

Our minds cannot tell the difference between what is vividly imagined and what is real, which is why we feel afraid watching a scary movie or cry when the hero dies at the end.

We know the person on the screen is just an actor, but for that moment when we are watching the film, the death we are viewing becomes real and our bodies respond appropriately with tears and grief.

Suddenly, in this moment, I am reminded of a friend, who many years ago, chose to take his own life. They phoned me because they found credit card receipts stashed around his apartment. My name and address were on them.

"He sent me gifts," I told them.

"He shot himself in the head last night," they responded. "Actually, two nights ago. The neighbor called the police when Jon's pals from work wouldn't quit knocking on his door."

I remember him as being a particularly ecstatic man. He used to talk about things like science and the sky and the beauty of life; the words tumbling off his tongue in an outrageous, ravishing manner.

He used to take aerobics classes with me and do these grand movements in the opposite direction. He'd go to the left when we were all going to the right. He'd smile and shout, "Woo weee!!" as the rest of the class silently plotted along.

He said the full expression of oneself was the key to creating a heaven on earth.

He said that to suppress anything within his soul was to die, one breath at a time.

I did not know Jon well enough to know why he chose to die. All I know is that he must have forgotten who he was, if only for one moment.

*I wish I could have been there to remind him,
as he had done with me when he sent me a bible with
the words, "I believe in you," inscribed on the cover.
I believe in you.*

I believe in you.

I believe in you.

And then...

I let go.

-Lysa Moskowitz-Mateu
November 29, 1999. 4:53 p.m.
Santa Monica, CA

ONE YEAR LATER....

November 20, 2000

There is an inability to put into words that which I long to say.

I grieve for the people I have lost.

I grieve for the people who are no longer here; here in the way we are accustomed.

I grieve for the souls who no longer walk the earth, the souls we no longer have the privilege to see, feel, touch, and communicate with in the most direct and forthright manner.

Why?

Why can we not turn back time?

Why can we not bring back those whom we love so deeply and shake them and tell them and hold them and allow them to know, truly know, that everything will be okay.

I grieve, just as you, for the ones who got away, the ones who chose not to stay.

I grieve just as you for the times we never spent, the love we never shared, the words we never said.

I miss my friend Charley. I miss him so much. Last night I wrote to his father asking for a tape of him just so I could hear his voice

Just one more time...

I want to hear his voice and see his face, the way it used to be.

I want him here, dammit!

I want him back!

And even though the connections I have made from here to the other side have offered others and myself, enormous comfort, right now I don't care. I want him back, for I too have a hard time comprehending the irreversibility of life.

With all the knowledge and experiences I have had in contacting the other side, with all the proof and accuracy in which messages have come through, even with all of that, I still want him back.

You still want your children back.

Your father.

Your mother.

Your friends.

Your spouse.

You do.

I know you do.

And it's okay.

It's okay to want.

It's okay to grieve the loss of not getting what you want. It's okay to fight the tears when others say, 'It's enough,' and then allow them to flow when you say, 'No. It isn't.'

Today I grieve

For the lost souls who could not find their way

For the people left behind

For the unanswered questions

The pain

The heartache

Today I grieve for what could have been

For what never will be

I grieve for the times well spent

For the things I didn't say

For the love I kept locked away

Today I grieve

Allowing tears to fall silently upon my face

I do not wipe them dry

I grieve for the wanting

The begging

The praying

The pleading... that things could be different

I grieve for the turning back of time

And the impossibility to do so

I grieve for the pictures I form in my mind

Of the people who are no longer here

I grieve for the ones who tried to reach us

For the signs we did not see

Today I grieve for you my friend

Today I grieve for me.

A butterfly lights beside us like a sunbeam
And for a brief moment,
its Glory and Beauty belong to our World.
But then it flies on again
And though we wish it could have stayed,
We feel so lucky to have seen it . . . .

Where the Journey Takes Me....

It has been exactly one year, almost to the day, since I first channeled *Conversations with the Spirit World*. The book sat on the shelf for that time.

I have not.

This journey has led me to places of which I could not have formerly imagined, places where I am tested daily to trust the words, thoughts, names, details, and places that come through me.

You see, nearly six months after the completion of *Conversations*, my life radically changed. I became that which I profess to be in this book – a channel for all those who have crossed over, to speak through.

It began at a book signing held by noted medium and best-selling author, James Van Praagh.

May 2000

Seated in the audience, I raise my hand. I hope he calls on me. I have so many questions to ask. Like why do my hands sweat before I'm about to write or why do these names keep popping up in my head?

He calls on me.

He tells me that spirits use the hands through which to relay their messages, the hands and the voice of those who are willing to speak their words.

"You are a medium," he continues. "You are a very gifted medium who has been a medium for many lifetimes. There are many people who need you out there, but you must first get out of your own way.

Once you do… you will take off."

After this, I made a little flyer about my services and waited for the phone to ring. It did. And suddenly, I was doing the thing that I loved to do.

I was a medium. I was helping people connect to their loved ones who had crossed over.

At first, I didn't trust everything that came through. I would get a name. A feeling about the way the person died, but I would keep it to myself for fear of being wrong.

It was my husband who taught me to just give out whatever I got and pay no attention to the ego part of me that demanded I be right all of the time.

I was doing a service for people. I was there to help them heal. As long as I focused on that, everything would be okay. And it was. For a long time, it was. And then another milestone occurred.

I decided to join a live answer community where people could call me for my services. I had never done phone sessions before and I was afraid. How will the spirits know who is calling? What if I make a total fool of myself?

My fears were quickly put at bay as the spirits came through with more clarity and precision than they had ever done before. I got full names, dates, private details about their lives and was able to have two-way conversations between the person on the phone and their loved ones who had crossed over. They were able to ask questions to which they, not I, knew the answer.

I began to receive thank you letters and notes of profound appreciation.

Then, I went on the radio. Star 98.7 asked me to do channeling on the air where listeners called in to receive spirit messages.

I prayed to my spirit guides to come through for me and they did – with flying colors. The response was enormous and since that time, I have had the privilege of working with many, many wonderful souls – both here and on the other side.

Recently, I made contact with a man who is currently in a deep coma, and has been for the past three years.

This was one of the most profoundly moving experiences of my life. Never having done this before, I allowed myself to get out of my own way and make a clear and open path for his words, impressions, visions, and feelings to come through.

The phone session lasted two hours and beyond speaking to her husband telepathically, bringing through details of his accident, his life, her visits to his hospital, I brought through details only he and his wife would know, and others, she would later confirm.

She got to hear, through me, what her husband needed in order to decide to return.

To wake up.

To come home.

She got to hear how much he appreciated when she wore a certain blue dress and how much he loved her kisses, three in a row, she gave him on his lips.

You see - No one is truly gone.

They are only visiting different realms.

There are many.

Earth is one.

And for us to want to stay in this realm, we must do certain things.

We must tell the truth.

About who we are

how much we love

how much we care.

Each time I do a session, I am awakened to the awesome miracle of communication that occurs with all living things, especially animals.

Tonight a woman's dog came through. Misty. When the woman asked if the dog was with her father.

The dog showed me a pristine attitude and told me, not in words, but in feelings, that she was not with him, but he was with her. Then the dog showed me herself under the woman's bed. So I relayed this message. The woman said, "I have Misty's ashes under my bed." And then she thanked me.

And then she cried.

The healing that occurs during these sessions is enormous. Questions are answered. Tears are shed. Love is exchanged. Hearts are healed.

And it is a first step toward asking, understanding, and knowing, that all we have is this moment... and this one... and this one...

And to use a moment of your life for anything other than expressing and receiving love, is to waste it.

We are here to use our time well.

To have our lives matter.

To leave our light of love so bright so that all who have the privilege to walk in our path feel warmed by our sunshine, moved by our words, touched by our hearts, and appreciated by our souls.

Capture Your Life.

You are here for a reason.

Set Yourself Free.

You are meant to be here.

Not in the future.

Not at some later date.

Now.

You are meant to be here - Now.

And how do I know this?

Because you are here.

And you are meant to shine.

So Go Do It

Get Out There

Live Out Loud

Laugh

Love

Lighten Up

I Love You

All of You

And I Love Me

♥ *Lysa Moskowitz-Mateu*

OPEN THE DOOR
TO THE OTHER SIDE

In your private session with Lysa, you will be offered the chance to connect with loved ones who have crossed over and be guided to learn how to tap into, preserve, and replenish your own individual power.

Using her clairvoyant, clairaudient, and clairsentient abilities, Lysa puts you in touch with the choices you have made and offers you the opportunity to experience the truth about who you are and why you are here. She empowers you to move forward.

The result is clarity, inspiration, and a purpose for your life.

Your Appointment is Waiting for You

Call 3 1 0-8 2 0-0 7 1 1

www.channelingspirits.com

LEARN THE SECRETS OF MEDIUMSHIP IN THIS EXCLUSIVE AUDIO SERIES!

<u>BUILDING A BRIDGE TO THE OTHER SIDE</u>

Is an amazing audio course designed for you to become your own medium by learning how to connect with your loved ones on the other side.

You will gain access to the unique signs, symbols, and messages spirits use to communicate with you and you will learn specifically what they mean and how you can use them now!

Plus, you will get an inside look on what really happens in the mind of a medium while she is channeling spirits!

This amazing course, designed to help you develop your inherent psychic and mediumistic ability, is **only $13.95**! If you order now, you will receive a special edition, signed copy!

Order online now at www.channelingspirits.com

Or call 310-820-0711